ESSENTIAL VOICES

BORDERLESS

Maria del Guadalupe Davidson, Series Editor

John C. Harris, Series Editor

David Monk, Series Editor

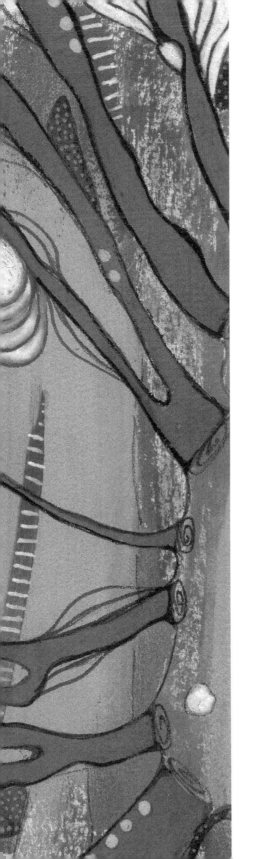

ESSENTIAL VOICES

A COVID-19 ANTHOLOGY

Edited by

AMY M. ALVAREZ

PAMELA GEMME

SHANA HILL

AND

ALEXIS IVY

West Virginia University Press
Morgantown

ISBN 978-1-952271-88-5 (paperback) / 978-1-952271-89-2 (ebook)

Library of Congress Control Number: 2022051300

Cover image: Detail from "Hold Your Breath," Michal Mitak Mahgerefteh, 2020
Cover and book design by Than Saffel / WVU Press

For the Uncounted

The imagination can inhabit the meaning of a single human calamity, but multiply it across an entire population, and the mind is overwhelmed. . . . One must tell either a small fraction of the story, by implication diminishing the whole, or one must attempt to take it all on and find that language itself cannot carry the burden. Historians revert to statistics, while literary writers may be inclined to find a different story to tell.

—Catherine Belling, "Overwhelming the Medium: Fiction and the Trauma of Pandemic Influenza in 1918"

CONTENTS

———

FEAR: *It lives in droplets*

DISTANCE: *As we moan into the phone*

MASK: *A parachute that catches my breath*

LABOR: *Warnings on the floor*

CONTENTS

SICKNESS: *My stomach charley-horsed*

GRIEF: *Interjected like a comma*

CONTENTS

SURVIVAL: *Remember every surface you touch*

JUSTICE AND RECKONING: *Colonial co-morbidities*

ENVIRONMENT AND PLACE: *Let the river turn the stone*

HOPE: *Beyond sorrow there's a gardenia tree*

LIST OF ILLUSTRATIONS

———

FOREWORD

I am thankful to WVU Press for the opportunity to create the Borderless series with my colleagues John Harris and David Monk. Our goal with Borderless was to make space for scholars, artists, and community workers who were interested and invested in the work of decoloniality, transborder solidarity, coalitional politics, and grassroots approaches to inquiry. I am honored that Amy, Pamela, Shana, and Alexis chose the Borderless series to publish this important anthology. I thank all the contributors for sharing their time, intellectual labor, and reflections on how the COVID-19 epidemic impacted (and continues to impact) their lives and communities.

The work of justice continues.

In solidarity,
Maria del Guadalupe Davidson

PREFACE

———

Until recently, the Spanish flu of 1918 was a pandemic forgotten. It began in the midst of World War I and the burgeoning Modernist movement in art and literature. At that time, writers and artists were engaged with novel forms of expression and experimentation that felt essential to a new era. The experience of the flu itself was far from "modern." The Spanish flu was a looking back, a turning over the shoulder to a past littered with plagues—yellow fever, polio, cholera, and other myriad diseases. Modernist writers and artists, while impacted by the pandemic of 1918, chose not to create work that referenced their experiences because it did not fit within the narrative of modernity.

As the world faced the threat of a new global pandemic in late 2019, the lack of creative documentation of the events around the Spanish flu in Anglophone literature presented a challenge: How were we to mourn a crisis of this magnitude? How could we avoid the mistakes of the past? Where should we turn to for comfort? Where were the stories we could turn to in our fear? Where were the voices of the marginalized—those most vulnerable to infection and loss?

As the editors of this anthology, we wanted to do the work of turning back for the sake of future generations. We also wanted to provide a space for individuals of diverse nationalities, races, ethnicities, sexualities, gender expressions, socioeconomic classes, and levels of confinement to tell their stories and document this moment not only from the Global North but from a multitude of voices, lived experiences, and perspectives from around the world.

As editors, we spent the first year of the COVID-19 lockdown seeking creative writing and artwork from people who may or may not have considered themselves artists. What moved us to compile these works was our deep desire to present work that was not represented in popular media. In the many special COVID-19 editions of literary magazines and anthologies that we observed coming out during this time, most were from artists soliciting artists and not necessarily centered on the marginalized voices of essential workers, people experiencing incarceration, Black, Indigenous, Asian, and Latinx people, LGBTQIA+ folks, those with preexisting conditions (both mental and physical), and those outside of the United States and the Global North.

The title of this anthology, *Essential Voices*, was inspired by essential workers, laborers unable to take time off or to stay safely quarantined at home and were instead forced to work under the threat of disease and potential job loss in order to keep the gears of capitalism churning. For example, contributor Ben Gunsberg's piece "Line Speed" points out that the Trump administration put many workers in the difficult position of facing job loss, lack of access to COVID testing, and risk of infection. In many US states, the sudden uptick of the incidence of COVID-19 was driven by those working in meatpacking plants. But other vocations were affected too. In Canadian glassworker Z. S. Roe's fictional work, "These Hands," he describes the conditions of a glazier business and the inherent risk of its workers contracting COVID-19. Such pieces build upon the evolving nature of work in the midst of the pandemic. Many workers are now pushing back against a system that prizes stock outcomes over their very lives. In the United States, the minimum wage has been raised closer to a living wage, but it's taken a pandemic and hundreds of thousands of lives to move the needle.

One of our primary goals for this anthology was to understand the experiences of the incarcerated. In a moment when so many felt confined, we wondered about what it was like for those lodged in the maw of a justice system that is not focused on the rehabilitation or even survival of the incarcerated. Our call was met with an array of experiences. Contributor Christopher Blackwell shares his story of getting married in prison during a time of safety protocols so strict that he could barely touch his new wife. In her letter to us, Alyce Copeland describes feeling safer in prison during the pandemic than she might have felt at home.

Our submissions from imprisoned people were primarily from US citizens. Many of their pieces were handwritten and mailed to us because the submitters did not have access to a computer. They were told about this text by creative writing instructors and teachers who work within prison walls. We have presented one of these handwritten works in our final chapter in its original format to showcase the limitations incarcerated individuals face.

During the pandemic, some individuals who were incarcerated were discharged early to mitigate COVID-19 outbreaks in these dense population settings. The formerly incarcerated joined those who were unhoused as a result of job loss, eviction, untreated mental health issues, and other reasons. The voices of those experiencing homelessness were difficult to access. We placed calls in shelters and regional newsletters to gather submissions from unhoused individuals. But how does someone without access to a computer or even a home address submit their work? Since we were not able to gather work from these individuals, the experience of houselessness was represented by photojournalists like Tom Darin Lisky or those who work as advocates or provide health care, like Robbie Gamble, author of the essay "Barriers." The inability to access works from this community showed us that despite our best efforts and the efforts of others, many narratives will remain unseen and unrecognized.

In addition to the health crisis that was ravaging the world, there was a racial reckoning within the United States (and elsewhere). The experiences of Black, Indigenous, Latinx, and Asian people in the United States have long been fraught, but the manifold experiences of these communities—all fiercely hit by COVID-19—has been one of extreme difficulty.

The deaths of Black people at the hands of the police have been a terrifying reality for millions across this nation. The Black Lives Matter movement has been in existence since 2012 when the death of Treyvon Martin at the hands of a self-appointed vigilante devastated African American communities. However, what was new in 2020 was the outpouring of support, both nationally and internationally, from people of multiple ethnic backgrounds after the death of George Floyd was captured on video by seventeen-year-old Darnella Frazier. This moment happened in the midst of the most terrifying days of the pandemic and came at a time when the United States was starting to wake up to the many injustices Black people have faced in this country, including the 1921 massacre that occurred in Tulsa, Oklahoma, when white residents attacked Black residents, destroying their homes and businesses and murdering their children. As Liseli Fitzpatrick points out in her poem "we've been here before," racism remains problematic and stretches back to the beginnings of settler colonialism.

Indigenous/First Nations people were hit hard by COVID-19. The loss of elders to the pandemic was not only a loss of history but of linguistic and cultural memory. The public was also becoming more aware of the brutality of Native American boarding schools, which existed until the early twentieth century, and the horrors of young children ripped from their families and forced to attend the schools. According to Harvard scholar Joseph Kalt, casinos and other tribal businesses, which represent a large portion of the Native American tax base, closed due to COVID-19. This in turn has directly affected access to health care for Indigenous communities where disease prevalence and mortality have been proportionally higher. Deidra Suwanee Dees's poem "Em Ontvlecetv / Invaded" encapsulates the multilayered heartbreak of COVID-19 within her community.

Within the anthology, Latinx writers have touched on the impact of COVID-19 and Immigration and Customs Enforcement (ICE) on their communities. We had hoped to acquire works by detainees at the US-Mexico border, given the draconian rules implemented by the Trump administration in 2016. As COVID-19 overtook the focus of the nation, the spread of disease at the already horrific border camps was rarely discussed in the press. While we only received one submission that was a first-person account of the horrors of ICE, a moving piece titled "My Uncertain Story" by a young person named Noe Hernandez, this essay serves as a reminder that, even now, young people are enduring prison-like conditions at our nation's borders.

Asian communities in the United States also have faced horrific violence since 2020 as individuals attacked Asian people of multiple ethnic backgrounds and nationalities, blaming them for the outbreak of COVID-19. This was exacerbated in the United States by former President Trump's derogatory, false, and racist comments. There is a pattern in US history of brutal tactics against Asian communities, including Japanese internment camps, the Chinese Inclusion Act, and the murders of Chinese railway workers. Our youngest contributor, Elia Min, a high school student, describes the increased racism during 2020 and how Korean food provides a source of comfort to her.

Contributors from outside of the United States offered a more global perspective as the waves of COVID-19 hit countries in different ways. In the opening chapter, Frances Ogamba's piece "The Worst of Times" outlines how Nigerians were affected by the pandemic and the subsequent ramifications for individuals. In one short story set in Nigeria, "A Story of Constantine, COVID-19, and Pandora" by Waliyah Oladipo, a woman being treated for hepatitis C and facing stigma from her family and community goes on to test positive for malaria while in the midst of the spread of the coronavirus. The work of these international writers emphasizes the shared global experience of COVID-19 and highlights the challenges that various nations face as we all fight this disease.

For individuals in the LGBTQIA+ community, especially gay men who survived the AIDS epidemic starting in the early 1980s, there were stark parallels with the COVID-19 pandemic—people dying without assistance or loving family members around them, and the desperation for a cure. Anthony Fauci's role in addressing the AIDS epidemic was explored in Joan E. Bauer's poem "I Cut Up My Hillary T-shirt to Make a COVID Mask." We also chose to include older poems, such as "New Age" by Robert J. Levy, which demonstrate the pandemic's parallels to the AIDS epidemic. The knowledge and support brought forth from this epidemic and community was crucial at the outset of COVID-19.

Preexisting health conditions were amplified by COVID-19. Joan Goodreau's haibun "Wish You Were Here" considers neurodivergence as the speaker communicates over Zoom with her son. In Catherine Young's piece "Invisi dis ability in COVID Times," she muses about her years of wearing a mask prior to the pandemic due to illness and what it is like to wear one in 2020. Phrieda Bogere's poem "Nudge," touches upon the epidemic of mental health issues that were intensified through isolation and quarantine.

While all of these voices were essential to the diversity of this text, our approach to organizing this anthology was driven by the expression of its contributors rather than by the segregation of their voices. Writers and artists touched upon universal themes, organized by chapter. Many were experiencing the same things but in different locations and levels of intensity. The sections of the book provide a cognitive chronology and cycle of the experience of the pandemic one year in. Parallel to the stages of grief, the chapters move from Fear toward Hope, passing through Sickness and Grief, an inevitable reckoning with Justice, a desire for Touch and Nature, and the insistence of Survival.

We layered the multiple ways of experiencing these events in each section by bumping the experiences of the aforementioned voices up against each other to provide a depth of understanding of the physical and psychological tolls the pandemic has taken on all of us.

Conclusion

We want this text to assist readers in making sense of COVID-19, to document the multiplicitous experiences of the pandemic throughout the world, and to help induce social change through the understanding and compassion that come through deep engagement with literature and art. In this regard, the work we have compiled is important in the near term. But it will also provide a source of information for future historians and policy makers. We see this anthology utilized in classrooms, by book groups, and as a historic document for future generations to understand the complexities of the pandemic during the geopolitical circumstances of the early twenty-first century. We envision discussions of this text that revolve around racial justice and reckoning, the prison industrial complex, health care, labor rights, and the environment.

As we write this, new variants of COVID-19 continue to spread across the globe. We intermittently face threats of outbreaks and a return to the shutdowns of 2020. The average age of patients presenting with the virus in current hot spots is becoming younger as variants show a new ferocity. As of August 2022, nearly 68 percent of Americans are fully vaccinated, but there is a continued politicized resistance to being vaccinated within the United States, even as people are desperate for access in other countries.

This anthology is meant to represent a point in time rather than a summation of the pandemic. These texts stretch from the earliest whispers of global illness and testing for the virus to Black Lives Matter protest marches during the summer of 2020 and the beginnings of impromptu vaccination centers in early 2021. We hope that the voices here and the era they document provide a space to contemplate the challenges we currently face and provide wisdom for those who may face these challenges in the future. May those future survivors learn from our missteps, be guided by our best impulses, and find comfort and courage in these words and images.

—Amy M. Alvarez, Pamela Gemme, Shana Hill, and Alexis Ivy

ACKNOWLEDGMENTS

———

The editors would like to thank West Virginia University Press and the individuals associated with the press's Borderless book series for their support and input with this anthology. We would like to especially thank David Monk, Sarah Munroe, Sara Georgi, John C. Harris, and Lupe Davidson for their support and positivity.

We would also like to thank Hannah Gittleman for her initial input and Laura K. LaGrone and Nyala Tafari for editorial support. We are particularly grateful not only to our contributors but also to the hundreds of submitters who bravely shared their work with us and made our final selection process exceedingly challenging.

Finally, we are grateful to our friends and family who have been of great support during this time, especially our partners and spouses: Jared, Richard, Richie, and Santos.

FEAR: *It lives in droplets*

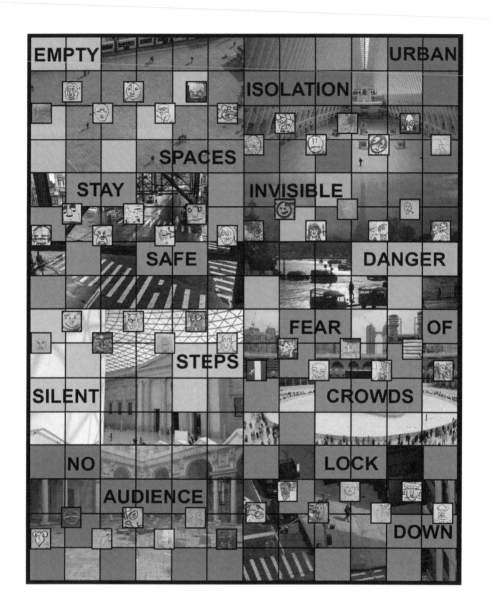

"THE GREAT EMPTY," DIGITAL COLLAGE · JODY ZELLEN, 2020

MONSTER UNDER ME

———

For you, my name isn't really important. What is important for you to know is that I believe in monsters. You may laugh now but, after I say my peace, let's see if you're still laughing.

In my twenty plus years on this side of the wall one thing has been drilled into my brain, toughness. Prison is no place for the weak. You gotta be tough; your body, your mind, even the way you dress. It's all about being tough, what we call hard. You gotta be hard. Never let the enemy see weakness of any kind and never, never, involve the guards. If you have a problem, you tell the big homie and he'll decide how best to handle it. This is the way that it is, this is being hard.

My cellie and I were pretty close; brothers from other mothers, some would say. We shared food, and the occasional illegal drink. I'd let him use my creased-up shirt for visits so he could look *hard* in the pictures with his girl and family. When he started sniffling one night, I asked, "You good?" "Yeah, yeah, I'm good," he responded. He slept on the lower bunk and would wake me with the sniffling and growled breathing. He was like this for two days before I suggested going to staff. He vehemently refused and thought I was crazy for even suggesting such a thing. He tried to laugh it off, even though I could hear it, the raspy dry thing inside of him. It was day forty-two of a lock down and I thought hard about who he could have been in contact with. We get a shower every seventy-two hours. During that time, he could have spoken to any number of the homies. The doors aren't solid, so you breathe in what comes out of that cell. It could have been the recirculated air. My eyes went to the vent blowing on us, its stale air having been in every cell at one time or another. Below me, my cellie sounded like a growling beast. He started coughing and his breathing became erratic. In the dark of night, I jumped down off the bunk. "Hey, man," I shook him. "Hey," I said louder. He clawed at me, growling, spittle flying from his mouth. I pulled away and moved to the light. When I turned back again, my legs wouldn't move. My Bunkie, my friend, my brother, was bleeding from the mouth and his breathing labored. He tried to sit up but was struggling. "What?" I hear myself ask. "What!" His clawed hand gestured toward a brown state cup. He motioned as if knocking, then I realized it was not a knock but a bang. He wanted me to bang on the door with the cup. This would alert the guards. Never, Never, involve the guards.

My cellie, my friend . . . My brother is no longer here. He died of COVID-19. I am no longer hard.

"ANXIETY," DIGITAL COLLAGE · ILARIA CORTESI, 2020

Poetry | *Rasha Abdulhadi*

TABLE OF CONTENTS FOR A MANUAL OF PANDEMIC RESPONSE PROTOCOLS

———

---

1   Darakshan Raja, 2020

How to keep yourself and others alive in america[2] ....
How to keep yourself and others alive in palestine ....
How others keep you alive ....
How to turn desolation into liberation ....
How to take escalation as opportunity ....
How to renew your rebellion ....
How to be careful, very careful, more careful than
    you've ever been ....
How to feel the domino of your somatic body ....
How to suspend the risk of your first and last true life ....

Previously published in *Mizna*

2   Kiese Laymon, 2012

THE WORST OF TIMES

———

A feeling that defies description taps me awake and settles deep in my chest as if I inhaled a blizzard of smoke. Updates pour in from my WhatsApp contacts—blinking across the phone screen with urgency—about Nigeria's first case of COVID-19. Panic flashes, like a struck match, in my vision. I picture the new death quickly pervading our airspace, stealing puffs of oxygen from reach.

The virus always felt distant when it ravaged China's Hubei province. I peeked at the damage through the windows of the internet: deserted streets, a lone silhouette of someone standing at the balcony of a building's fourth floor, a body lying still in the cold. It is devastating to piece together a new reality that appears at the same time, remote, even when we feel directly linked to it. Through those weeks, the cloak of distance severed me from fully feeling, protected me from crumbling. I merely imagined, willing a pain I did not yet understand unto myself.

When it began to cross country borders, zapping across oceans to settle into crowded boulevards of Europe and the Middle East, I felt a little afraid. Its indeterminate nature was confusing as to what preventive measures could be effective. The speculation—it lives in droplets, and therefore lives in the air—implied that humanity was grappling with the worst infection in the new century. Yet the terror seemed afield and the supposition that the humid weathers of most sub-Saharan African countries would not let it in or let it thrive rang credible.

On this foggy morning however, with the clouds hanging low overhead despite the brilliant rays of a rising sun, the new death permeates our borders. The media ripples with opinions, rules that may serve to keep death at bay bandied about with fervor. The deep distrust most Nigerians reserve for the government of the day bars them from totally understanding or believing that the virus has come for us too. In response to the news, memes, as shocking as they are repulsive, strew the Nigerian social media. Their aim is to stir laughter, mocking the Nigerian way of life fraught with contact—handshakes, hugs, and every kind of touch with another human. My distress soars.

There is a union in our ways of living: between a rich man's house help and the sales attendant at the grocery shops, between the grocer and her barber, between the barber and his children who play with other children in the community. This awareness defeats the logic that the infection is a "rich people's illness." I renew my daily hope that the fire will be stubbed out from somewhere before the burning coals smolder to the bottom. The tragedy I foresee, especially when I revisit the story of the influenza years of the twentieth century, yanks a groan out of me.

The panic wanes in March when the Nigeria Center for Disease Control (NCDC) announces that Nigeria has become virus-free. I chat with my friends Kay and Mau about how relieving it feels, especially because we all have young children. Perhaps my worry runs deeper because I also have an old mother and close relatives who have crossed well into the danger circles of the virus. Most of them struggle with underlying illnesses—high or low blood pressure, mild blights on the liver, prostate cancer, diabetes.

As life picks up with the usual gusto, a plane carrying passengers from countries already neck-deep in the pandemic cruises into the Murtala Muhammed International Airport in Lagos and launches all the passengers into our fragile society. The tweets from the National Centre for Disease Control, asking for over twenty passengers to isolate themselves for two weeks fetches me a new kind of grief. I wonder how community infections will be managed if the airports are not properly manned. There is little or no existence of orderly urban planning in most Nigerian states. Will the NCDC be able to identify the muddy street I live on, or reach the family that lives in the hovel next to mine if something begins to go wrong with all of us?

My mother argues the virus's existence with the obstinacy of a septuagenarian. She insists that her guardian god would weave a cloud of protection around her. I labor to explain to her the importance of going out less and stocking foodstuff. The only way to dissuade her from attending the Sunday masses is to fill her in about the deaths in Italy. "Even the pope has taken to isolatory masses," I tell her. "How can a virus be effective in God's house?" she asks in utter confusion.

I feel helpless yet pricked with the need to change the world around me. When the government takes too long to shut down schools, I pull my toddler out of preschool. I rant on my Twitter page and on my WhatsApp status. My heart pulls apart at the seams. "We cannot handle this! We cannot allow this dirt to fully settle!" I scream unending. There are yet no acceptable levels of testing. Rivers, the state I live in, will have to transport samples to Edo, another state lying some two hundred kilometers away. The reality is too burdensome to analyze.

In April, some state governments set up makeshift gates to protect their boundaries and control interstate transmission. The families living and working in different states are suddenly stuck on different sides. This unexpected alteration to our normal way of living reminds me of historical walls that severed families in North and South Korea, and in Berlin. I imagine the horror of having a wall grow between loved ones. I worry for our survival if these separations become permanent.

Major markets are soon shut down, and only street shops are authorized to stay open. Food suppliers, however, get stuck at the state boundaries and I switch from the fear of the virus to the fear of hunger-induced deaths. Prices inflate by 50 percent. Sellers start hoarding their goods.

After the new curfew laws are set up, many stranded travelers litter the entry points of states. On the ten o'clock news, I see a woman on national television lying spread-eagle in the middle of the road by a state boundary. Fear wraps me at first, because she appears too still to be alive. When her lips start moving, she says there was terrible traffic on her journey from Nasarawa to Abuja. "I have not eaten or taken water. No hawkers anywhere." The image of her body twitching weakly to produce words leave me troubled for many days. In her, I see my mother. What if my mother lies somewhere, suffering from thirst, and I am stuck in another location, unable to reach her? I wonder which is fair, granting the woman entry despite flouting the curfew or abandoning her. Is it fair to drain out lives just to fight the pandemic?

There is an upsurge of police violence in communities. Reports of point-blank shootings for as much as playing football in open streets trend on Twitter. I find photos of a little girl cradling her dead brother. I see this image for a while, like the image of the woman lying at the state boundary, flitting in and out of my vision. We are not a people to be shut in. We share a kinship with the wind, therefore it is difficult to stay still. It is tasking to drill social distance into our people because we thrive on contact with others: in wine bars and hotels, at weddings, at funerals, in our neighborhoods, in markets. How can we stay away? My life is suddenly hung on telephone chats. Some of us find a way to rope around one another without touching.

I feel connected to all the deaths occurring everywhere on the world map, to all the erasures. Instead of the nameless hundreds, or the identical coffins that unify the dead, I wish for some sort of identification—pictures of victims, even names, published globally and paid final respects. Even that, I am aware, amounts to nothing. A mere scratch against the pain.

In May, the Rivers state government imposes a total lockdown on Port Harcourt, where I live, because of the rising toll of infections, and authorizes only pharmacies to stay open. "Do you take medicines on an empty stomach?" a neighbor asks me. The starvation that soon follows appears more critical than the virus we are preventing. I run out of pepper and salt, and resort to saltless meals, while assuring myself that it is a healthier diet choice. The house walls grow in on me. I yearn to run outdoors and stroll along the road. To see people. To be seen. "Waiting is inextricable from expectation. To wait at the mercy of another person, place, or thing—it implies need," writes Ayden LeRoux in *The Art of Stillness*. Despite having been grounded in the experience of isolation (I work remotely), the hallways of my body burst with conflicts of nearness. My diseased tooth rattles in the stillness and my muscles twitch. Often violently. The days bear a bleak taste as each one comes and goes. It becomes needless to know what weekday it is. This feels like incarceration, a friend tweets. My food stack slowly vanishes, and in my lack, I imagine many poorer families crumbling to more lack. I also visualize the older generation taking ill because of the separation from their community.

The Port Harcourt lockdown is eased a few times—for Easter, for another weekend, and for the Eid. I see a people drenched with paranoia and the ambition to hoard food and money. The bank queues stretch past their gates despite the shortage of cash. The network is overlabored with online transfers and many of the transactions end up unsuccessful. In a few hours, the shelves at superstores are stripped of tissue papers and provisions. My eyes fall on a woman who meets an empty shelf. She gasps and slumps on the store's balcony, wiping her eyes as if ashamed to have me witness her agony. Algae-infested loaves of bread begin selling at double the price, and a hungry, panicked crowd buys them off display shelves around the city. Good taste suddenly becomes a privilege. We begin to crave meals that do not have to be decent.

––––––

I am paranoid, waddling within the precincts of my fear for safety—from the spike in robbery attacks blamed on hunger, the lack slowly ravaging my food store, and a breathing virus that might live inside a loved one, plunging us all at risk. I become especially fastidious. It takes a lot of effort not to act squeamish in the midst of people who pay little attention to the times we are in, who dismiss the tragedy as a distant business of the West. I demand that my nephews sanitize and also wash their hands when they visit. It irks me that they choose to visit at such a time, an unfavorable time to mark friendships and familial relationships. My fear is palpable throughout their stay. I tense up as they play with my son, knowing it is useless to ensure any sort of safe distance between them. If any of us have the infection, we all might contract it. I wonder often at the callousness of it all—that I have become afraid of children who usually excite me with their visits. What does it mean, this desire I nurture for their distance and absence? Why am I more concerned for my safety than their wellness? This is perhaps where the seed of abandonment is sowed, where the culture of lonely deaths begin.

Outside our domiciliary comforts and worry for jam-packed food pantries is the fear of medical emergencies. The ordeals of Italy and Spain fuel my fear. The rules of medical emergency have been rewritten by the virus. Apart from the NCDC-authorized isolation centers, Nigerian hospitals are not empowered to treat anyone with the symptoms. Medics usually flee in the face of a probable case, abandoning the patient to their fate. My family friend who suffered from dyspnea (labored breathing) since the birth of her fourth child is refused treatment at a government hospital. Her husband is received by empty hospital lobbies and fleeing medical staff. Her symptoms bear a similarity to COVID-19, and for this reason they do not touch her. Three hours later when the hospital matron on duty finally arrives and is willing to attend to the sick woman, she has gone cold.

Through these months, I have been so deeply disturbed by the experiences of others that I cannot remember what mine have been, except for the panic crisscrossing my mind at every turn. I possess an excessively imaginative mind that stipples dots without my consent. The woman's avoidable death creates a large canvas in my mind where I paint many other victims who died merely because they needed medical help in the time of COVID-19. Many more headlines stream into my phone—a pregnant woman dies after being detained by the task force for moving after curfew hours, an elderly woman dies in isolation even though she does not have the virus. I am on the brink of something I cannot name. I swipe most of the news updates away without clicking on them.

What the pandemic looks like around me is different from what is happening in some parts of the world. We do not have trucks queuing out of our cities, filled with dead bodies. We do not have coffins lined up at the centers. Disparate from our ways, illnesses and deaths have become private. Grief is hidden. This is spurred by the fear that a patient's evacuation from the arms of their loved ones might be the first chime of separation. Worse, families are denied the final viewing of the corpse, a highly placed tradition in most Nigerian tribes. It is important to us to mark burial spots. Unmarked graves are as disturbing as the loss of a loved one.

People hide coughs and reports of high temperatures. Cloves of garlic and ginger roots become highly sought-after commodities. Teas are brewed from lemongrass and scent leaf as the new alchemy to any COVID-19 related symptom. Some victims of the virus die far away from the government's eye, surrounded by their loved ones and a community who may easily be at risk. People grow a thick front against the times, insistent that the virus is merely an advanced strain of our usual malaria and typhoid fevers. Yet I fear because I know too much not to.

My mother calls me to complain of a morgue overflowing with dead bodies in a nearby town. Funerals have been banned by the government since March. There is a shortage of formaldehyde, a chemical that preserves dead bodies from rot. The putrid smell eases into nearby neighborhoods, pushing people out of their houses.

Burials in my tribe, Igbo, are performed—a celebration of affluence and success—which smoothens the healing process for the bereaved. These performances were at first postponed because the bereaved families were hopeful that the chaos would last only a short while, hence the congested morgues. Burials are nonetheless carried out without the large community gatherings or the colorful zest that accompanies final farewells. The state governments issue guidelines on how to grieve, a strange alteration to our normal. Two of my uncles die in the thick of the lockdown and are thrown into the ground in their sleeping clothes, without the well-polished shoes or the ceremonial white lace that corpses are wrapped in for public viewing. It is hurtful to witness. Most of our family members are locked away in distant states by the boundary closures, missing out on the honor of shoveling the sands of goodbye into the graves. It is a wrong time to die, many Facebook posts say.

Past the empty markets with the rusty perforations on their zinc sheets, I inhale a faint green scent which can only be fresh vegetables. The smell of other wares that used to be on display crams into my nostrils. The new absence is like a passageway leading to our shortcomings, shedding light on our selfishness and clamor for wanton gains—on security personnel scattered across communities, demanding bribes to allow passage. This is ongoing despite the job losses and closed businesses, despite the general inability of people to get food.

I remember the deaths in the early days of the virus. I have a rote memory of the daily toll in the world. I check the charts daily because I do not want to forget. A terrible thing is happening to the human population and I forbid my heart to feel numb around it. *You need to protect yourself*, Mau tells me on WhatsApp. Despite my utmost desire to be a witness, I have built the courage to look away from the numbers. My memory has become compressed like those of the people around me. Mourning is tiresome. As I free myself from its clasp, I too begin to forget. Hand washing now seems laborious. I visit a hairdresser, breaking the rules of social distancing. I touch surfaces and forget to sanitize my hands. I clamp down the thought swelling in my chest that the possibility of a widespread infection is creeping close. Have we all become inured to the new death? Are we all waiting in line to be killed? The panic of the first few weeks is now a distant and temporary thing. How do I breach familiarity between my toddler and the strangers he bumps into when we walk along the street? Can we tell who has it?

The lockdown and the interstate boundaries have been eased, but the virus has not. The number of infections rise daily, spreading faster because of our inability to stay away from others and the desperation to hunt for food. I am afraid I have become the community I once abhorred. I have now been prodded deep into the logic of people around me. We are all living one day at a time. *All die na die*, they reiterate, and I have lost the grounds to argue it.

ESSENTIALS

———

One week before shutdown, the gaping mouths of
empty store shelves set my eyes ablaze.
    Items we normally have at our fingertips, elusive as dust.
Pandemic continues and I duck it by turning to online.
    Prices peak as panic sets in.
Don't call it rationing. Too many memories, all of them bad.
    Instead, signs cry, *two per customer*. Hundreds of us need
        our share.
The grocery site can't deliver for 5 days. The food ran out today.
    Six feet apart, people snake around the grocery store lot
        waiting to
be allowed in. The food bank looks worse.
    The world is upside down. They said two weeks two months
        ago.
Sleep is a memory, while dreams are fierce. Sometimes, they walk
    during the day.
    I remember Grandma kept cash in her mattress, cookie jar,
        underwear drawer.
I need a stash in case the market crash is permanent.
    The bankers won't answer. I am a red light flashing
on their old push-button phone.
    I pack plastic gloves and my last can of Lysol to make my
        withdrawal.
I kiss my son goodbye and let the TV babysit him. He is afraid to
    be outside.

Dozens of cars got to the bank first. Dozens of hands
pressed each key.
I spray down the ATM before I take out my cash.
I ain't trying to leave here with anything I didn't come here
with.

Poetry | *Linda Parsons*

RECIPE FOR TROUBLED TIMES

———

Throw it all in the pot—the war and hunger
years, the Depression's hoboes, pandemic
pandemonium, Irish potatoes gone black,

the half-eaten chicken born to be broth.
Add the six days your father stopped eating
in the nursing home, enough was enough

of this tough old life—and the seventh
when he feasted alone. Hidden pockets
of fat, gristle, the delicate ribcage

and scrawny wings, tender pickings
at the joint, splintered drumstick
you gnawed at your grandmother's table,

little tail she called the Pope's nose.
Cook it down, thick with rising fever,
chills, isolation. Add elderberry tea,

onion poultice, kerosene, both comfort
and thorn. Cover the mirrors when
it lightnings, nail the quarantine notice

to the doorframe—red measles, diphtheria,
whooping cough. Throw it in with
time's slow burn, watch it boil over.

You endless glutton,
you soup of consequence,
you bowl of glistening meat.

Previously published in *The James Dickey Review*

NIGHT GUARD

———————

Who knew my dreams needed reining in,
galloping symbol and precipice, until

after decades of TMJ, my jaw began to crumble,
like so many these pandemic days

who clench and grind, crack molars and fillings.
I click the new night guard in place to stay

the bone loss, though at 3 a.m., I spit this
foreign bit on the extra pillow, ride on

unhaltered. I dream no fear at the departure
gate: shoulder to shoulder as in my old life,

breathing the same air, off to the Midi-Pyrénées
near Toulouse, along the ancient pilgrimage—

but there's a summer snow, at least a foot,
and I didn't pack boots. My parents would

send them, but they're off being new incarnations,
and I'll never again hear their voices—

DiMaggio's fly ball at Sulphur Dell, nutmeg
not clove in the cobbler—except the wishing

voice in my head, mouth locked in stasis. I'll never
know whether night guards or hogties me,

lathered to the brink of prayer, staying neither hope
nor haint, whether the watches hover until

I awaken, or if, in the wee hours and more gnashing
of teeth, I can't help myself and spit it out.

Previously published in *Cold Mountain Review*

PANDEMIC PANDEMONIUM

———

Pull that thing up over your nose
so you don't become exposed
slowing the spread reduces the dread
CDC has failed us over and over
letting science be defeated by assumptions

Transmission of the plague
due to lockdown tactics
Millionaires and billionaires
wealth will not secure their health

Since there was no buffer everyone had to suffer
Safely discontinue isolation once you recover
There's a whole lot more going on in this world
than what you see—pandemic has all of us panicking
creating a worldwide pandemonium

Symptom-checking forms are part of the new norm
The outbreak is the straw that broke capitalism's back
Virtual hearings prove that we are taking this seriously
214,000 no longer stand says Johns Hopkins University

10 day quarantine
has all of us acting mean
Disinfect it! Clean that place up!
This pandemic pandemonium
is messing all my plans up

Poetry | *Robert Okaji*

EVEN THE ROBINS KNOW

———

The world has soured and nothing I touch
will return it to before. Even the robins
know this. Or especially the robins.
They've lost their babies to chance and
fear amidst the helicoptering maple
pods, and now the barren nest glares
at us when we slink past. I enter
the store with other masked shoppers
searching for yeast and tissue, alcohol
and beef. Or hope. We wander apart,
silence weighing us down, sharing
in avoidance our discontent. I want
to scream. I want to wake up, having
been a player in someone's dark, acidic
dream. Look, I say, though mostly
to myself, we live the same lives.
Can we no longer laugh? Or talk?
And those devastating little pleasures—
smiles now lost behind cloth, our
fingers accidently touching—will
they slip back into place someday,
like a fledgling returned to its nest,
forever altered yet still viable, capable
of breath, of empathy, of song?

DISTANCE: *As we moan into the phone*

"LONG-DISTANCE LOVE," DIGITAL COLLAGE AND ILLUSTRATION
ILARIA CORTESI, 2020

Poetry | *Xiaoly Li*

HOW CORONA EVOLVES OR MAKES US EVOLVE, OR WE HAVE TO EVOLVE TOGETHER

———

—video chat with Mom on a hazy, snowy day in March

> *Are you all staying home now?*
>> Yes, our poetry group meets online.
>> We have five hundred people meditating twice a day at
>>> home at the same time.
>> And we only take walks in our neighborhood.

> *Don't go out, just do tai chi in your backyard.*
>> We walk the opposite side of the street when people pass
>>> by.

>> China is the safest place now, do you go out?
> *We still stay at home. A manager calls every day to check our*
> *temperatures. We need to persist.*

> *What are you eating, do you get things you need?*
>> Rice-millet porridge, walnuts, Brazil nuts, pine nuts, and a
>>> Fuji apple.

> *Don't go to stores.*
>> These were home-delivered and left in our front door.

> *Soak vegetables in soda water to keep them clean.*
>> Oh, good idea, will try.

How is our granddaughter in the hot spot of NYC?
    We have pleaded and she's not coming back.
    She said she can concentrate better on the work over there
    and prevent cross-contaminating us.
    And she wants to read more books in evenings.

Does she stay at home and learn to cook herself?
    She works from home but jogs along the river.
    And we told her to make ginger, lemon, and honey tea.
    Sometimes we shop online for her to grab a delivery time
        slot.

    She used to dine out. Look at this photo of what she has
        made last night!
Wow, very impressive. Roasted chop,
red peppers and asparagus, fresh colored and shining.

Do tell her to not go out and to exercise at home.
    We can't keep warning her.
    She wants to hear life's other stories.

Previously published in *North Meridian Review*

Poetry | *Joan Hofmann*

SEQUESTERED ALONE

I want to
touch
your face
yet I'm not to
touch mine
either. I still
want to
touch you.
Not to
be able to
makes me
want to
even more.
I owe much
to ones who
have touched
me before.
I take nothing
about that
touching
lightly, for now
I'm insatiable.
When chance
comes I
will let you
stroke or rub
or even pinch

me. I just
want to
be able to
touch you.
Let me
touch you.

TO WHOM IT MAY CONCERN,

———

My name is WF5098. That is who I am to the state of California. I used to be a housewife by the name of Alyce Copeland. I am 68 years old and now reside at California Institution for Women (CIW). Ironically enough, when I was first incarcerated, I lost everything I owned and everyone near and dear to me. As an inmate, being isolated from the world like we are has turned out to be a blessing in disguise. If I had still been living in that senior citizen complex, I'd bet a nickel to a doughnut I'd be dead by now. It appears that nature was using COVID-19 as a way to cull our excessive population by decimating the aged and infirmed right off the bat. . . . First and foremost! I look at it like this, I no longer worry about paying rent, having enough food, medical care, and just check out all the wonderful protection we have! No, I'm doing okay right where I am AND in fact made the decision to stay right here and I can't be evicted!

———

You call it a cell
me institutionalized?
I call it a room.

"MANIBUS," PHOTO COLLAGE · VERONICA SCHARF GARCIA, 2020

Poetry | *John Cuetara*

LOVE IN THE TIME OF CORONA

———

What's safe sex when
the virus is ringing our bells
and trying to slip inside
with the groceries,
when a kiss or even a
breath may be our last?
All that's left is love
through the wires,
a telephonic affair
in the darkness,
a slow seduction alone
together listening for
sighs and zipper sounds,
undressing on faith
and meaning it as
we moan into
the phone.

———

Previously published in his book *Mixed Messages,* Big Table Publishing

WHAT WE KNOW ABOUT THE FATALITIES

———

"I can't remember the last time I dreamed," Anne admitted to Evelyn with the phone on speaker. She poured a gin and tonic in a glass that looked like a chemistry beaker, a graduation gift from their mother. The only clean glass in the place.

Evelyn called too late in the evening, as usual. But she'd just got off the phone with her dream therapist, as part of her "recovery process" from the last break up. Liam the defense attorney with a secret family who lived outside the city on an acreage. The wife had their thirteen-year-old son call Evelyn a few months ago with an assault of details. "I guess I'm not as in touch with my intuition as I thought," she'd said at the time to Anne.

She went on: "Anyhow, the dream therapist told me I need to look into deepening my understanding of my family of origin. I've been dreaming about Liam's wife. We are on a plane together over an ocean, but I know it's the Atlantic and I know we were going to Scotland."

"Okay, and . . . ?" Anne sighed.

"Anyhow my therapist says there's maybe a desire for me to reconnect to my roots, how we never knew much about Dad's family. And that was somehow manifesting in my relationships."

"Sure." Anne rubbed her eyes.

"Like maybe we should go to Scotland. When we can travel again. Maybe we can take Mom."

"Mom isn't interested in Dad's family. I can guarantee you that."

"I'm sorry, I've got to say, Anne. You're not dreaming, not processing things . . . you need to start therapy, like, immediately."

Anne snorted.

"What? I have a lot of resources I can pass on to you."

Evelyn attributed Anne's nocturnal dysfunction to a lack of sleep, shift work, stress. Seeing all those stabbings and gunshot wounds and car accidents. The boy jumped off the school roof (seeing that seemed to especially rattle Anne). And now the virus.

"Well, you're right about the fatigue," Anne slumped into a lazy lotus position on the living room couch, setting the beaker onto the glass coffee table.

"When was the last time you went on a date, I mean even before everything was locked down? Don't you feel physically blocked as well?"

Anne had no answer. Evelyn wondered out loud if there might be long-term damage, emotional consequences. Anne almost fell asleep, sliding down the couch, eyeing the gin, untouched in its clear dewy glass.

"I'm fine. I just need to make it through this week."

"But isn't that every week, Annie?"

"Then I just need to get through this year. Or two."

———

The attending surgeon was telling his favorite story, about a rectal foreign body he treated when he was a resident in the eighties.

"I said to the patient," he said, laughing at himself. "He's . . . ah . . . he's got his ass up in the air and my hand's in up to here." He wrapped his thick fingers together above his wrist, his belly pulling at the fabric between the buttons on his white coat. Drops of dried blood in an archipelago across his sleeve.

"I said: 'Sir, you may've lost your dignity, but at least we've found your car keys.' And I held them up and jingled the damned things!" He wiped his eyes with the back of his hand. "And goddammit if that guy didn't bring me a bottle of scotch to the emergency room the next day." He slapped the top of the table with his palm and knocked over a long-abandoned Starbucks cup, sending a wave of pale brown coffee down the center. The medical students looked at each other, wide-eyed and with distress as the coffee crept toward the far table edge.

The residents around the table laughed. Anne laughed, later than the others. She was not really listening. She could recite the story herself, having heard some version of it regularly over the past three years. The smell of the cold coffee was nauseating, but it made her crave caffeine.

"Wow, Dr. Burrows. It must have been wild back in the day," chuckled Brian, the fifth-year resident as he looked at his phone. He was tracking the price of Bitcoin on a cryptocurrency app.

"The things you could get away with back then, eh?" Dr. Burrows winked at the students as he left the conference room.

Brian, still focused on his phone, let the team adjourn for the day. The room emptied quickly, leaving Anne and one of the medical students, a long-armed freckled kid with dark red hair that looked almost green under the fluorescent hospital lights. The student tried to mop up the puddle of coffee with a stack of stiff brown paper towels. Anne folded her arms on the tabletop and laid her face across her bicep. She closed her eyes. Just for a second, she promised herself.

"You shouldn't touch the table with your arms like that. It's a fomite," he said.

"Thanks, Kevin," she sat up, shaking herself awake.

"My name is Alex."

Brian stopped her in the hall on the way to her locker to change. "I know you want to get out of here. You look terrible."

"Gee thanks, Brian."

"But I forgot to round on the stabdomen on GH3 that we admitted over the weekend. Can you go discharge him if his pain is under control without narcotics? I think he's homeless, but the social worker can figure all that out."

A nurse scrutinized Anne silently from the desk as she dressed. She took a fresh surgical mask from a box on the dressing cart in the hall and placed it on her face. She tied on a neon yellow fabric gown, with two strings behind her neck, crossed two ties around her waist, cinching the baggy cloth tight. She pulled purple disposable gloves up over the gown's floppy cuffs.

Anne knocked gently on the patient's door and pushed it open. The room was dark. The lights were off. The patient's view through the window was obscured by a brick wall erected for the new dialysis unit.

"James," she said from behind her mask. "Hi. It's Anne from the surgery team. I'm here to take a quick feel of your belly." Her voice was artificially sweet, an automatic compensation for her fatigue. She walked toward the bed. "If you're feeling better, we are going to let you go home!"

She leaned over the patient. She could see he was small and slim, not much taller than herself. He lay with his head dead center in the middle of the pillow, his face turned up to the ceiling. The light from the hospital TV screen glinted off of his skin in the semidarkness. She could see that his light-blue surgical mask had been pulled down below his chin.

"Mr. McLean." She grabbed his thin shoulder. "James." A cell phone rested on his motionless belly.

He was quiet. Anne searched his throat for a pulse. Then his wrists. She shoved the TV monitor toward the wall, where it was anchored by a long metal arm. It struck with a bang.

Anne searched the wall above the bed for the light switch and pressed it. In the light, she saw that his face didn't match his adolescent frame, with deep lines punctuating his thin mouth and a ribbon of purple scar up the right side of his neck. His brown eyes were open and unblinking.

"James," Anne dug her thumb hard into his shoulder. He didn't move. She leaned over the bed and ground her knuckles into his narrow sternum through his blue patient gown. He didn't flinch, didn't moan. The hair stood up on her arms.

She stumbled into the hall. The nurse was on the phone at the front desk. She pointed stiffly at Anne.

"You have to take your gown off in the room," the nurse shook her head.

"Call a code," Anne felt sweat build between her skin and her surgical mask.

"What?" The nurse hung up the phone.

"Room 22. He has no pulse. He's GCS 3. I can't rouse him."

"Are you sure?"

"Yes, I'm sure." Anne scowled behind her mask.

Anne went back to James. She pulled the surgical mask up over his nose and mouth and started chest compressions.

The nurse entered, put a gloved hand to James's neck.

"I've got nothing."

"Get the code team in here. Now." Anne snapped.

The nurse ran into the hall and yelled toward the front desk: "Call a damned code, Janice!"

The call went out overhead and Anne was only partly aware of it: code blue GH3. James's belly undulated as Anne pushed her body weight onto his chest one and two and three and four and one and two. She stood on the balls of her feet to leverage more force. She felt the cartilage between his ribs bow under her hands, the sensation of bone cracking. His abdomen undulated with each compression and a shadow of blood appeared down the midline, breaching bandages atop his skin.

"You okay? You need me to take over?" The nurse asked.

Anne heard the code team's clamor in the hall, with its hurried voices and rattling carts of equipment.

"No. I've got it."

———

The sky was dark by the time she got home. She parked in the lot down the street from her building and walked past the centenarian ash trees and elms lining the sidewalks in front of the painted brick houses, some boasted turrets, nearly all with peaked dormers. The street was quiet, with only a faint bleat of sirens drifting over the buildings from the main boulevard.

She approached the front of her apartment building, a set of wood and scuffed brass doors under a date stone in an old font: 1918. A man she didn't recognize held a door for her. He was tall and fine-featured, in a dark slim suit and black tie. He had a cigarette between his lips. No sign of a mask. She shook her head, declining to pass through the span of his arm as he kept the door ajar. Instead, she propped the bottom of the door open with the sole of her foot and waited for him to pass.

He nodded and smiled, raised his eyebrows. It was nothing personal. She nodded back with a short glance: you don't want to get near me.

Anne found her neighbor Trent standing at the top of the stairs, near the antique stained-glass window with its Easter green lilies and red diamonds, the glass gathering in a slow corrugated wave toward the bottom of the wooden frame. She called him Trent the Psychic though the business card taped to his mailbox suggested he preferred the titles *Spiritual Counselor* and *Life Coach*. "You know," she'd recently heard him say through the door to a client, "I'm only six credits short of a social work degree."

He wore an orange scarf around the lower part of his face. His arms were crossed tightly. He paced toward her.

"You're standing too close." She stepped back, almost off the top stair.

"Dr. Carpenter . . . can we talk?"

"I told you to call me Anne. What's going on?"

"Sorry. Yes. Anne." He shifted his weight nervously. "My throat is killing me. I don't have a fever or a cough, but I can barely swallow."

Anne smelled a sweet, dusty incense coming out of Trent's open apartment door.

"Call your doctor. See if you can get tested."

"Do you think I should be worried? Can you take a look?"

"Trent—"

"I saw a guy on CNN, around my age, in New York. He had had a sore throat. And maybe asthma? No fever. They found him dead on his couch after he didn't come in to work." He was muffled by the scarf, but she heard his voice tremble.

"There are many reasons why you might have a sore throat. Don't assume it's the virus. Have you been isolating?"

"Yeah, I've only been seeing clients over the phone. Doing readings online."

"Then go back inside. Call your doctor."

She walked down the hall to her door.

"Birds, Anne," Trent said, clearing his throat.

"What?" She turned back to face him.

"In your apartment."

"What does that mean?"

"There were birds living in your apartment, maybe budgies in a cage. I'm getting a 1900s, 1920s kind of feel."

She rolled her eyes and turned to put the key in her door.

His voice cracked. "If you hear birds singing, it's because they're happy you're here. They've been waiting for you. I thought you should know."

"Stay inside. And turn off the TV."

Anne closed her door. She stripped and rolled her clothes, including her underwear, sports bra and running shoes, into a careful ball, which she placed gingerly, like a small radioactive animal, into a black garbage bag. She ran naked to the back door and slung the bag out onto the back fire escape. It slammed into the previous day's bag of soiled clothes.

She rubbed the doorknobs—front and back—with disinfectant wipes and hurried to the bathroom. She turned on the shower, scrubbing her skin methodically from her neck to her feet with a bar of hard white soap, the kind her grandmother bought in bulk. She washed her hair, her fingers and shoulders stiff with fatigue. She stood under the water with her eyes closed, planning to stay until the hot water ran out.

Then Evelyn called.

"It's too late," Anne said without a hello, dripping water across the bathroom tiles.

"It's barely ten," Evelyn snorted.

"I have to get up at four-thirty. I worked until eight. I'm exhausted. And a guy just died on me."

"I'll be quick."

"Did you hear what I just said?"

"Maybe you should have a drink."

"You know I'm trying to cut down."

"So about Scotland . . ."

"I'm hanging up."

"Shush. I've been working with that therapist and I decided to do some research into the family tree and I ended up on one of those genealogy sites."

"Ev—"

"Have you eaten today, by the way?"

"Not really. I haven't had an appetite lately."

"You sound like you have low blood sugar."

Anne wrapped a towel around her wet hair. Evelyn kept talking so Anne put her on speaker.

"Anyhow I ended up talking for a couple of days online to this second cousin of Dad's, on his mom's side. Jean. She's sending me a bunch of hundred-year-old photos. She sent me a scan of one from her phone. You wouldn't believe it."

"What's that?"

"Dad's grandma looks just like you. It's eerie. She has your hair. Your cheekbones."

"Huh."

"And her husband was a carpenter! What a coincidence!"

Anne smiled. "Okay, that is creepy!"

Evelyn laughed.

Anne walked to the front window adjusting the towel knotted above her breasts. She watched the man in the suit smoking on the building's stone bench. He put his hands through his dark hair and then dangled an arm along the back of the bench. Like he was daring someone to come sit next to him.

"So, did your dreams give you any insight into Old Liam?" Anne asked.

"Would you believe that he called me yesterday?"

"Of course he did. He's an asshole. I assume he's stuck at home with the wife he's been cheating on and they're homeschooling their four kids and he's going crazy. I've got to go to bed."

She fell asleep in a towel atop her duvet. The light from the hallway fell across the foot of her bed, onto the textbooks scattered across the floor. Her long dark hair lay in heavy wet clots around her head, her mouth open in a yawn, like she was hungry for air.

Later that week, Anne was presenting to the team on morning rounds: an eighteen-year-old girl who had driven her father's car into a tree after a party with alcohol and benzos on board. She had a broken arm, broken nasal bones. Fractures in her skull around her eyes. Anne was just about to propose to Dr. Burrows that the patient be put on oral pain medication when her phone rang.

"Come on, Anne, we're almost done here," Brian grunted. He'd been on call all night. His eyes were half-closed and his light brown hair was visibly dirty.

Dr. Burrows stared at her. Anne took the ringing phone out of her scrubs pocket and looked at the display.

"It's a call from inside the hospital. I should probably answer it."

Anne turned away from the team and lowered her voice, staring at the hallway floor in front of her. "This is Anne with General Surgery."

"Anne Carpenter?"

"Yes."

"This is Sandy from Occupational Health and Safety at the Misericordia Hospital."

"Yes, I'm here at the hospital too."

"I need you to confirm that you were part of a code three days ago. A patient named James—"

"McLean. Yeah." Anne sighed.

"Yes, on GH3. He was tested postmortem for—"

"The virus?"

"Yes and he was found to be positive. As you are probably aware, our protocols require that you be tested as well," Sandy said in a monotone.

Anne tried to swallow but her throat was tight.

"You are required to self-isolate until you are shown to be negative with no symptoms."

"Okay."

"Please go home and limit contact with others. We will call back with a plan to test you."

Anne dropped her phone back into the breast pocket of her scrubs and turned to Burrows.

"That was Occupational Health. I have to go home. The guy who died on the ward the other day was positive. I was there for the code. I have to get tested."

The team stepped away from her, almost in unison. Brian stumbled backward into a group of IV poles and sent one crashing to the floor. Alex, the student, shook his head subtly.

"On this ward?" one of the off-service residents asked, wincing.

"Yeah."

Dr. Burrows shrugged. "Well, then. Go home. Brian, I guess you're going to have to stay and cover the OR this morning." Brian groaned.

Anne walked toward the door at the end of the hall. She didn't look back.

She slept until it was dark. She woke up, her hair still damp from the shower. She checked her phone. No calls. She called the number for Occupational Health. Busy. She slept through the next day too. She ordered pizza and asked the delivery guy to leave it in the hall. She made another round of calls: more busy signals.

She was studying the surgical management of liver injuries on the couch after dark when Trent knocked on her door. She watched him through the peephole. He was pacing, his face covered with a black cloth mask.

"Anne. I know you're home, Anne. I need to talk to you." He banged on the door again. "Please? I'm freaking out!"

She waited for him to walk back across the hall. She went quietly into the kitchen and cracked some ice into a large metal thermos, then flooded it with gin and tonic. She dressed in yoga pants and a sweatshirt, her only clean clothes, and sat on the back step. She looked at the bags of dirty clothes and took a long drink.

"You ever go up on the roof?" A man's voice startled her. She flinched.

"Jesus, you scared me."

She squinted up into the security lights at a dark-haired figure leaning over the railing.

"Remember me? Guy from the door?"

"No, I've never been up there."

"Why not? It's supposed to be the best thing about this building."

"I don't have a lot of spare time."

He came slowly down the fire escape, the old wood creaking under his weight. He was wearing a black sweater and dark, expensive jeans.

"You look like you need to get out for a bit," he said.

"I don't think so." She shook her head.

"Come on. Check out the tree." He smiled and showed perfect ivory teeth.

"What tree?"

"Someone put a palm tree up there a couple of weeks ago. It's a whole thing around the building. Might be worth a trip, no?"

She took another drink and shuttered as the cold bitter tonic flowed over her tongue. She could hear Trent pounding her front door and his dampened voice. She looked at the man and shrugged.

"Okay. One moment." She quietly topped up her thermos and closed the back door carefully.

They walked to the top of the wooden fire escape, then climbed a ladder that clung to the brick facade like a tenuous and rusted vine. He went up first. He landed hard on the roof, then held his hand down to pull her up. She slowly accepted his palm into hers.

"Still not into chivalry, huh?"

"People shouldn't be touching each other so casually." She wiped her hand on her sweatshirt. "The whole physical distancing thing."

"Don't you think that's a bit overblown."

"In what way?"

"It's a lot of hysterics, right? It's not as bad as they say."

"The virus?"

"Yeah." He took the thermos from her grasp and drank.

Anne felt her lip curl. "You have some special insight into this?"

"Just common sense. Things are never as bad as they say."

"And what's your area of expertise?"

"Meaning?" He lit a cigarette with a silver Zippo. His thick black hair fell over his eyes.

"What do you do for work?"

"I'm a lawyer." He pushed his hair back from his face. "Come and see the tree."

Anne inspected the palm tree set in an oversized terra-cotta pot, ringed by a half-moon of mismatched lawn chairs and an empty wine bottle. Someone had taped a handwritten note to its trunk. She leaned forward to read it, using the light from her phone. *No cigarette butts in the plant you trash heaps!!* A wind chime hung up in the palm fronds moved in the night breeze.

"What kind of law do you practice?" She sat in one of the lawn chairs. He sat too close, right next to her.

"Criminal law."

"Oh, a defense attorney?" She smirked.

"So you have me figured out, eh?" He scuffed his shoe along the tile beneath the lawn chair.

"I might."

"I've watched you scurry around your apartment naked for the past three months. You're not that advanced." He teased.

"Is that when you moved in?" She felt her cheeks burn but refused to look away.

"Working tomorrow?" He leaned toward her in his chair.

"I am definitely not." She smiled and drank out of the thermos.

"Oh, did you get laid off?" He gave her a pitiful frown.

She didn't respond.

"Listen, I have some pretty good gin down in my apartment. The Botanist. I've got a whole cabinet full of scotch too. You want to come down?"

The man's phone rang. He looked at the display and stood up.

"It's the cops. Gotta earn that dough." He winked and took the call, turning his back to her.

"Yes, this is Will Spence with Brantford Atwater Temelkoff." He nodded. "Yes, he is my client." He flicked his cigarette onto the concrete. "And what are the charges tonight?"

He walked toward the other side of the roof.

"So the assault charge is assault with a weapon? A knife? Okay, yeah I'll talk to him. Put him on."

Anne left the chair and leaned over the edge of the building. Beyond the streetlamps and darkened trees, she saw the cross atop the hospital. Its red light reflected in shards across the river as the water moved north in its cold spring crawl. She drank the last of the gin, the metal thermos numbing her bare hands.

She heard the man, fragments of his conversation from across the roof. "Don't say anything to the police. I will see you tomorrow for the bail." She pulled her phone out of her pocket. No calls about the test. But Evelyn had texted her a photo: a vague and faded sepia formal portrait of a woman in a stiff dress. She had distant eyes and curls down past her breasts.

Anne dialed Evelyn's number.

"Well, well, well . . . what did I do to deserve a call from the busy Dr. Carpenter? Why aren't you in bed?" Evelyn teased.

"Long story."

"Okay . . ."

"Yeah, so that photo you sent. I guess we do look alike."

"You finally looked! Her cheekbones, right? And her hair!"

"Yeah. I forgot to ask—what was her name?"

"Davina."

"That's kind of pretty." Anne shivered. The night air moved her hair across her shoulders.

"Also, you'll think this is wild," Evelyn said dramatically. "I found out from Jean that she died of the Spanish flu!"

Anne felt the man's body behind her. He slipped an arm around her waist. Her stomach burned.

"I've got to go," she hung up on Evelyn.

"Sorry about that," he said. "I can't turn my phone off at night. It's like I'm on call."

"I get it."

"It's hard to explain, but sometimes I feel like this job is just me waiting for bad things to happen to other people."

She warmed her hand under his. He stood silently. Patient. She brought her fingers up to his neck. His skin pulsed under her touch. The warmth of gin spread behind her breastbone. The echo of sirens came over the river and from the dark trees, the sound of birds.

Previously published in *The Quarantine Review*

Poetry | *Diego Islas*

DO LOCKDOWNS EVER END?

———

Months, plural, of a lockdown,
sick of a smear of jelly and peanut butter.
Does it ever end? Seven times tested plural.
How many negative times does it take?

Trying to say sane, 24 hours a day, locked down,
wow! What a trustee camp. Cereal child molesters,
and murderer get one hour of recreation a day in
maxed security. I went to go feed 'em across the street.

Mental health, Oh! You can't buy more than $15
of food, and we won't feed you enough.
Either way, You're screwed and hungry.

No sunlight, just a dorm, and over preheating.
The guys with the windows don't want those
little bugs to blow into through the windows; keep it closed.

Does it ever end? Do the sleepless nights ever end?
Do the guards ever stop yelling? Will I get my mail
today or next month? Do we really get in trouble
for praying by the restroom?

Just another 24 months to go, on top of my
36 months done. Plural, Mom, I'm almost home.

Pretty soon

WISH YOU WERE HERE

———

"Wish you were here," I say to you, Ian, my grown-up autistic son. You watch me appear from the dark onto a small, rectangle screen. Do you recognize my frozen smile? My mouth moves in sync to metal words. "Ian, how are you?" No Answer. You stare at me from your supported living home where there's no visitor allowed, not even me. "How are you?" I raise my voice over the void that separates us. You look away from the sound and say, "Fine." "Great, thumbs up," I cheer. We mirror thumbs up. Our words are at an end. What more is there to say? I hold the small screen that holds you in my hand. We wave, both safe and well, but this Coronavirus Spring goes on without us. The blossoms fall on reflections of almond trees in the lake nearby. I wish you were here. Our screens go blank.

We would walk beside
almond blossoms, new goslings
silent together

COMFORT

As I walk through
concrete and steel
rubbing shoulders with those
un-allowed to feel
I try to seek out a bit
of comfort

try to find something
soft
a cozy place to sit
I find only concrete and steel

So I forget about my own
behind
put on different glasses
to get a different
feel

Now I see a social study

Have you ever wondered
where the awkward, quirky, anxious
unique, outside-the-box
girls end up?

The left handed
the unafraid
the poor
the hurt

The mothers of the children
acting up in school,
crossing the street
ALONE

They are here with me
at the cold, steel pay phone
raising their children
in 15-minute, long-distance
increments

They are here
standing anxiously
at four o'clock mail call
hoping for pictures,
proof that someone
is giving their children

a little comfort
a cozy place to sit.

Poetry | *E. Ethelbert Miller*

DIDN'T WE ONCE CALL IT LOVE?

————

What one misses most is the undressing of another
The lifting of blouse and shirt
The placing of hands on chests and breasts

One misses the touching that lingers before the kiss
The unmasking of tenderness
The moisture that floats between a lover's body and air

————

Previously published in his book, *When Your Wife Has Tommy John Surgery and Other Baseball Stories,* City Point Press, 2021

THE CHEAT

———

I.
If not for my partner I'd forget how to love,
how to let human in, how human feels
what *is* human.

II.
I hugged my mother once in June.
Before that it was February,
or was it December.

The next day, we learned
we might have been exposed
on account of someone else's affliction,
call it megalomania, or cocaine.

Either way, a condition or substance
that makes fathers become
figures of children's imagination
instead of dads that love the essence of their being,
the fact of their existence,
the thought of their joy.

III.
I remember the sole handshake,
Memorial Day. Just another day
to this conscientious objector,

except that handshake shook me
because I did not invite the
too-thin-white-male-stranger I later learned
was doing meth
to violate my invisible boundary,

to place me on the spot in pandemic
as Black and genetically hypertensive
as I feel, as I am.

I rushed for sanitizer,
tried to believe
that all my distance and mask
and glove and disinfectant
and months in isolation
were not erased the day
I stepped out into new world
to climb into kayak,
to meet lake, the Cheat,

where boat explodes
and drunk kids drown
without vest, without vessel,

my fear and a dread
that would go on to grow
like some invasive plant that takes over
every fiber of your being,

but you water it,
because it gives you something to care for.

IV.
Partway through paddle
the same kid, high from West Virginia,
"accidentally" pushed me
into my craft on a break off a dock
just as lake police jetted up to tell us
we weren't allowed to occupy
the planks of wood that seemed built
just for what it is that we were doing,
snacking, to replace what we'd burned
with the fuel to keep on.

My Achilles, sliced by plastic shard
from sloppy construction.

I went on to paddle another hour,
my beloved's shirt a tourniquet.

It bled for weeks.
Took months to heal and scar.

HOW I'VE SURVIVED THIS LONG, PART 3

———

CDC Tip: Hold your arms out toward the person next to you.
Your three-foot arm, plus their three-foot arm will equal the recommended
distance.

Of course it is strange to inhabit this earth,
only connected by the air we breathe.

If we all spread out across the world's landmasses,
our fingertips touching, we'd make a giant corporeal net—

a grid of electric human energy
upon which *anything* might be communicated.

A virus replicates—desires its host
comes into contact with another host. Honestly,

I desire the same.
What am I, if not a host for touch?

I'm unaware of what I carry within me. With my touch,
I convey consequence beyond what I intend-

fourteen days later, a death on the other side of the world.
And I'm unable to trace back along the web I created-

unable to trace myself back to the source.

———

Previously published in *The Healing Muse*

Essay | *Christopher Blackwell*

WHAT IT'S LIKE TO GET MARRIED IN PRISON DURING A PANDEMIC

———

On the day of our September 2020 wedding, my fiancée, Chelsea, and her best friend, Megan, were the first visitors to a Washington State prison—the Monroe Correctional Complex, where I've been incarcerated since 2003—since the COVID-19 pandemic ramped up in March.

Although we decided to get married last January and were approved in May, we weren't able to exchange vows until four months later. Tenacity on Chelsea's part, along with help from friends in the right places, including Washington State senator Joe Nguyen, got us that far.

But the challenges didn't end when she arrived for what had to be the strangest marriage ceremony ever to take place, in or out of a prison. While the pandemic has thrown weddings, and life in general, into chaos, the disruptions have been particularly acute for prisons and the people living inside them.

We expected to wed in a virtual ceremony, but the Department of Corrections (DOC) approved an in-person ceremony.

When Chelsea and Megan arrived, a guard harassed them about minute details. Both were stripped of their brand-new custom-made masks, even as another guard nearby had to be reminded twice of proper mask protocol. A measuring tape was even brought out to measure Chelsea's heels and dress—modest by any standard, and well within the guidelines provided to her.

Finally, after thirty minutes of badgering, an administrator—levels above the guard in the chain of command—stepped in to allow Chelsea and Megan into the visit room, where I waited with George, my friend, fellow prisoner, and witness to the ceremony. Without this intervention, it is quite possible Chelsea could have been turned away.

The large, square, harshly lit space hadn't been used in months. The tables and chairs normally used for contact visits were piled up in the corner, and the standard backdrop typically used for photos of prisoners and their visitors occupied another corner. They would serve as the only decorations for the ceremony.

Chelsea and I stared at each other through tearful eyes, searching for words of comfort. It had been six months and eight days since I had seen her. I was thankful to see her eyes, at least, even as the mask hid the rest of her beautiful face. But it couldn't hide the pain. We were navigating an emotional minefield.

Chelsea and I originally met years ago, when she was teaching a constitutional law class at the Monroe Correctional Complex. Years later, we reconnected through our criminal justice reform work—mine from inside these walls and hers from the outside.

When we decided to get married in January, I imagined this day much differently. Rather than six feet apart and masked, I hoped to be close enough to feel her breath on my face. As I stood there, finally seeing her in person, it was all I could do not to grab her hand. It broke my heart.

Frustrated and nervous, not knowing how the ceremony would proceed, we refused to waste even a second. We said how much we had missed each other and promised that everything was going to be okay. We must have said "I love you" a thousand times in those short minutes.

I wanted to hold her, whisper in her ear that everything was going to be fine, reassure her that this nightmare would soon come to an end. But the contract we signed in order to have our wedding meant an embrace could only lead to catastrophe.

Had we breached a six-foot distance, the ceremony could be terminated, Chelsea could be removed from my visit list, and I could be dragged to "medical isolation," which is essentially solitary confinement. We understood the need for safety measures, but the prison staff does not always abide by the same rules—an inequality that stings.

Our officiant, a chaplain who I came to admire for his unwavering devotion to prisoners, did his best to make the ceremony as beautiful as it would have been on the outside. We were blessed to have his compassion and love as he reminded us that we were now "one unit" that would move through the world together, despite our lack of physical proximity.

When it was my turn to read my vows, I choked up, barely able to read the words. I highlighted the love and empathy I had always experienced from Chelsea's kind soul. I pledged love and loyalty until the very end. In Chelsea's vows, she reminded me of the many strengths she sees in me and just how important it was to her to enter into a lifelong journey together. Her words meant the world to me—touching the deepest parts of my soul, one we now shared.

After the ceremony, we were moved one at a time to sign the marriage certificate, using pens we removed from plastic bags. After one of the prison administrators took a few photos, Chelsea was told it was time to leave. We cried as the realization hit: our time in each other's company was over, and we didn't know when we would see each other again.

I stood at the door that would lead me back to my six-by-nine-foot cell. Watching her leave, I could see she was crying, and I could feel the warm salty tears slowly streaming down my own cheeks. George was saying something about how amazing our vows were, but I could barely hear the words coming from his mouth.

This is meant to be one of the best days in a person's life, I kept thinking. I know we won't remember it that way.

I didn't have time to pull myself together before George and I were taken into a room to be strip-searched. It was an unnecessary humiliation: we were never closer than six feet to anyone from the community, and the ceremony was watched by five prison guards, two administrative staff members, and dozens of security cameras.

When I arrived back at my living unit, I was in a daze. I wanted to feel happy and excited, the way grooms on the outside felt—and to some extent I did—but overall, the experience was painful, humiliating, and hard.

Each time a friend in my unit asked how it went, I struggled to give an answer. Mostly, I responded with a shrug and said, "It was difficult." There really were no words for this, the oddest wedding that ever took place. This would not be a fond memory on which to look back. Instead, it was just another way the DOC—and our country's mishandling of the COVID-19 crisis—had stripped a special moment from our lives.

In my unit, there never would have been a wedding with cake or dancing, regardless of COVID-19 restrictions. But if the pandemic had been handled more responsibly, I wouldn't have been deprived of the ability to caress my bride's soft hand, slide the ring on her finger, and seal our vows with a kiss I had thought about and planned for months. Under normal circumstances, we would have been allowed to share the moment with friends and family after the ceremony.

While we are grateful to finally be married, it's painful to see news stories of people ignoring the pandemic, having large weddings and parties, while we wait indefinitely to be able to hold each other again.

I'm sure lots of people think we don't deserve to be married, but the Supreme Court has ruled otherwise, upholding prisoners' rights to marriage as fundamental. Those same people likely don't care that a day we should have been able to enjoy turned into a nightmare. But I wish they would consider the fact that most prisoners eventually return to free society. Allowing people like me to have strong, loving, and lasting relationships is not only a measure of basic human respect, but also helps make society safer. Making our weddings difficult was punitive, rather than restorative.

Our wedding was conducted with social distancing measures so strict that even a kiss to seal the marriage was forbidden, with the ceremonial placement of rings nowhere to be found. But it was still the moment we made a pledge to be together forever. And that is what we will hold onto.

Previously published in *INSIDER*, November 2020

MASK: *A parachute that catches my breath*

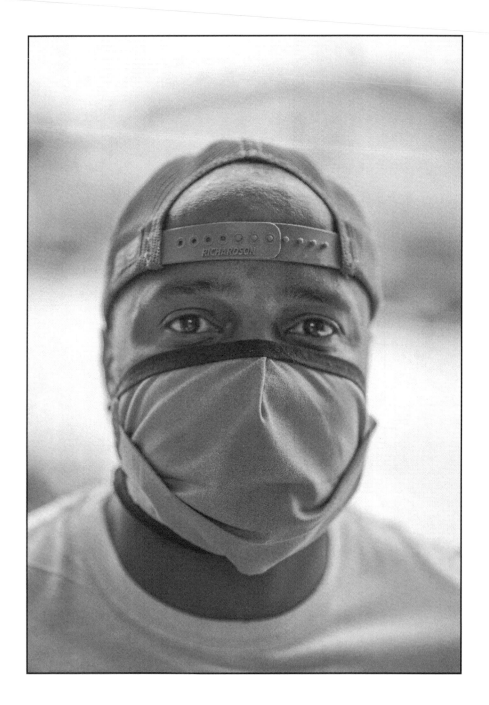

"RELIEF WORKER," PHOTOGRAPH · TOM DARIN LISKEY, 2020

Essay | *Catherine Young*

INVISI DIS ABILITY IN COVID TIMES

———

Before

Before COVID-19, I was likely the only masked person around in public for miles and miles. My life was lived in isolation with my family, and my rare social interactions and purchases took place outdoors in all kinds of Wisconsin weather, year-round. My disability is invisible, and its demands sometimes make me invisible as well.

For twenty-five years, I have worn a mask called "The Bandit," a triangular fabric with a neoprene and metal nose clip and an adjusting strap that ties around my neck. It is appropriately named. Before COVID-19, my mask frightened people. When I wear it, all anyone can see of my face are my eyes. Often my mask is hot and uncomfortable, and it makes it difficult for people to understand me when I speak—which I must do if I am in the rare position of purchasing something for myself. While wearing it for public transportation in the time before the COVID epidemic, I was greeted with wide-eyed stares, and sometimes questions about what illness I might give the people around me.

"I am not carrying a disease," I said, reassuring them. "No, I don't wear a mask to protect you from me—I wear it to protect *me*," I had to say. "I am disabled with extreme chemical sensitivity (MCS) and cannot be exposed to fragrances, body care products, cleaners, or molds."

That's the short list. A longer list includes anything derived from petrol: permanent markers and Sharpies, ignited paraffin candles, motor exhaust, plug-in or spray bathroom fragrances, asphalt, pill coatings, pesticides, plastic laminators, synthesized medicines, copiers, and mail—to name a few. My disability requires accommodations that people (including other disabled people) have difficulty understanding.

I have complete mobility; it's simply that I can't get in the same venue everyone else can without dire consequences.

Disability often partners with isolation—and my mask is emblematic of it. Wearing my mask pre-COVID, I would stand at the door of a store and signal someone to come talk with me so I could explain that I couldn't come in and what I needed. Wearing my mask pre-COVID, I would arrive at the entrance to an event that I had checked out by phone calls beforehand and I'd try to quickly get the attention of someone that a burning candle needed to be put out, or markers for nametags replaced by pens so I could come in. There have been many times in life where I have made a forty-mile round trip to an event or gathering only to discover that someone has used a substance lethal to me, and after everything I've done to make the long journey, I have to turn around and leave. The worst part is that likely no one would ever know that I was there or that there was a problem because no one came to the door to help.

Wherever I went, there was always the possibility that people in public would draw away from me, believing me a threat—especially parents with their small children.

Over time I discovered that I could reach out to the children who were asking their parents' about my mask. "Oh," I always said, trying to put them at ease, "I wear a mask because I get sick from things in the air. The mask helps me breathe. Can you tell if I'm smiling behind it?" And just for a second, I would pull the mask down and smile, and then pull it back up. Children always responded by nodding and smiling back at me.

———

I have always been a writer, and with the onset of my disability's isolation, I chose writing as my survival tool, finding ways to create, tell stories, and be published. I still longed for community, though, and I imagined that there could be ways for me to participate.

When I would contact conference leaders and ask to be connected remotely, I was often shrugged off. There was one exception—a week-long workshop with a university staff who saw remote participation as an opportunity for inclusion. The best they could do with the technology at the time was to hire someone in my workshop to shepherd an iPad remotely connected to me via Skype. The iPad was placed on a desk as part of the circle of workshop participants. The writer leading the workshop would call on me just like everyone else. Whenever I couldn't see who was speaking in the circle, the participant would self-identify. I became part of the group with jokes flying back and forth. I was even brought along to the dining hall so I could catch the conversations at the table. We built relationships. That weeklong workshop was a light shining at the end of a long dark tunnel. But the opportunity was a rare one. Though I continued to propose attending conferences remotely and leading writing workshops online, I was met with closed doors.

That used to be my reality.

In spring 2020, the spread of COVID-19 turned everyone's world upside down. Even mine.

As COVID Descended

In March 2020, I made the decision that I would break out of my isolation and travel 160 miles round trip to a house concert. It was something I hadn't done in over thirty years, and I felt that my health was stable enough to take the risk. For a few weeks beforehand, I was in contact with the concert organizer, asking my long list of questions and requesting that a few accommodations be made, such as no use of a gas stove while I was present. As our emails went back and forth, I was met at first with a patronizing unwillingness. I took my upset over the incident into my writing and created a piece about invisible disability, and then let it go.

At the last possible moment, the concert organizer contacted me saying that I would be accommodated. And so, on March 12, 2020, the night before the COVID shutdown in my state, I made my way to our capital to attend the concert. In my world of isolation, I often miss what everyone else catches on the news, and did not realize that we were all on the precipice of enormous change.

On the way to the concert, I stopped at a food co-op to find a snack. The store was packed. Everyone's shopping carts were filled, and the lines stretched into the food aisles. It looked as if everyone was shopping for a holiday feast. I thought perhaps it was what happens on Thursday evenings in a big city. Unbeknownst to me it was the day of the toilet paper panic.

At the concert, the beginnings of concern about COVID were filtering in, and concertgoers were asked to wash their hands at a table set up in the hallway—something I had to refuse to do because of fragrance and chemicals. I arrived in my bandit mask with several replacements for the length of the performance. I tried to introduce myself to people around me who eyed me warily. When the concert was over, I moved as quickly as I could out of the building into fresh air.

The next morning, when I revisited the food co-op for a road snack, it was completely empty except for workers quietly restocking shelves. By then I had heard the governor announce the planned shutdown of our state's schools and businesses, and I confirmed with a store worker what I had seen the day before was a panic.

I remember the shutdown that followed in spring as a time of darkness and uncertainty; a time when our family kept ourselves at home as much as we could, closely following news and interviews for answers. We watched videos recommending wiping down anything that came to the house—packages, mail, groceries—something that for my family had always been a routine requirement of my disabling conditions.

I received many calls from friends knowing how precarious my survival is with a compromised immune system. I could report that I was well because I was isolated as usual, and our needs were met.

The thoughts at that time were that COVID might pass in a few weeks—maybe a month. As it became increasingly obvious that we had no idea what was going to happen, some people got to work on making masks, and mask patterns became available online. Entrepreneurs created masks with all kinds of themes and designs. All at once, I was no longer alone as a masked person in public. Other adaptations quickly came along—restaurants and grocery stores began offering delivery and curbside pickup, services I had previously sought as accommodations. And when it really became apparent that we would be in isolation for the long haul, people in my life and many others across the world began accessing online real-time video platforms for sharing meetings, social time, conferences, performances, readings, and workshops.

Startling and strange, the COVID year of change has drawn some of us out of isolation and back into community. It has pulled me into engagements with other humans, allowed me to sit in an online group with a cup of coffee and have a conversation, or to attend poetry and prose readings. Most surprising is that the changes wrought by this pandemic have given me opportunities as a disabled writer in areas where I was previously shut out: chances to participate in readings and to lead writing workshops without any fear of my ability to be present in a space with workshop participants. During the time of COVID, I am leading workshops from the stability, security, and comfort of my home. And finally, I, who had been so isolated and invisible, have been able to come back into the world. I have a full schedule of engagements through platforms, and Zooming has become part of my vocabulary.

Disability and COVID

Part of human survival is learning from difficulties. I want to say that because of new adaptations for surviving COVID-19, we all have an opportunity to rethink inclusion for people often left out. I want to imagine we are beginning to see new ways of living.

Here's how I see disability and COVID.

Imagine a shuttle arriving at the door. The rest of the world is on it, including your neighbors, and they're heading to employment, shopping, recreation—all the activities of life. You're still scrambling out the door, but before you can grab your coat, the shuttle is gone. That was before the pandemic. Now with COVID, when you see the metaphorical shuttle depart, you look around to find there are many neighbors at their doors, coats in hand, staring down the same street as you.

When we talk about social and economic justice and inclusion, we need to pose careful questions and listen deeply to identify needs. By really listening to the needs, we can solve problems of barriers; we can welcome everyone to the circle.

COVID-19 is still a threat, and for me, the increased use of sanitizers in public makes life more difficult. And yet—*and yet*—I count my blessings. I have a place to live; I have the ability to communicate; I am no longer isolated. I recognize this is my particular experience, and many people in our country and worldwide are suffering. My wish for the future as we survive these COVID times is that we remember the possibilities we created for human community. Perhaps 2020 is the year we make a turning point in our understanding: that we are all here together, that we each need to be recognized and offered the opportunity to be included.

For me it has been hard wearing a mask these past twenty-five years and living in isolation, and I would not choose either if everyone modified environments so I could engage. Outside of a pandemic none of us would choose masks or isolation.

I imagine that I will always be wearing a mask. But perhaps the year 2020 is the year when mask wearing became another possibility of being a human on this earth. I first saw a glimmer of it late last spring when I went for a hike with my daughter.

A family with a teen was coming up behind us on a narrow trail. All of us were wearing masks, and as my daughter and I stepped aside for their group to pass, the teen startled me with a compliment. "I like your mask, "she said. "Where did you get it?"

She was smiling. I could tell.

CORONA SPRING

———

—*after Mariangela Gualtieri*

We did not make the sky. No. Nor the birds
that entrain and lift together in large numbers
through collective, intuitive moves. And we

did not make the moon, or the grass, or the
sand that falls through the hourglass as if
in our finitude we understood all the blessings

of time. so when it stopped, tied us
to our tracks, let flail and rail
on the hem of our thoughts,

something was wrought, something
new . . . to show us we make things
together. We do. We make the weather,

make children and dinner to share.
We offer the rice and the wine. It's not
that we have no power. Aren't we made

in the shape of our maker? We
stopped to discover new orders
keeping our distance from one another—

We enter our hearts, falling together,
pulling apart, tumbling out of the masks,
out of our minds that try to analyze,

to rationalize, blind as a bat
bumping its black fuzzy body
into the rafters of blame—

ratcheting down from the roof of the attic
where ancestral histories are stored.
We must play in this global game,

must unmask the dust and the dark
and dig down to dig up,
look for—and hold up the sky,

believing we also make light.

Previously published in *The Impossible* by Kelsay Books, March, 2021

UNMASKED

for what use are these words
when the end is skinned silence?

zooming into the dead pond
the camera smells suspicion

the woods went wrinkled
the red lips bleed black

adjusting the mirror, I see grass
growing over my neck and nose

let's bargain some civilization
and talk with our tongues sticking out

"JUGGALO BLM," DRAWING IN PEN AND INK · MICHAEL FOX, 2020

THE FABRIC OF SOCIETY

Nancy woke at eight o'clock on a day that was just like every other day. She rolled over and pulled her knees into her chest. Lying in a fetal position, she wondered if she should get a dog. Then, at least, she'd have a reason to get out of bed.

She sighed and sat up, pushing her feet to the floor. Reaching for her bathrobe, she caught a whiff of something gone bad. My god, was that coming from her? She lifted her arm and sniffed: old rotten chicken soup. Gross. When was the last time she showered? Tuesday, maybe? Yes, Tuesday, the day she picked up her medication. Nancy glanced at her phone. Tuesday was five days ago. Shoot.

This pandemic was totally destroying her life, including, it appeared, her hygiene habits. Since she rarely went out, she was finding it harder and harder to care about how she looked or even smelled.

Nancy was seventy-three, a widow with diabetes and rheumatoid arthritis. For many years, she'd taken a variety of medications that helped control her pain, but they also suppressed her immune system, making her particularly vulnerable to death by COVID. With this in mind, she was extremely careful to stay home and take safety precautions.

Nancy put on her robe and shuffled to the kitchen to make coffee. Every day, she felt more robbed. She didn't have that much time left, so she couldn't afford to give away a year to this virus. She felt increasingly deprived of everything she loved. Max, her only child, lived over two thousand miles away. She hadn't seen him or her three granddaughters in months. FaceTime was not a good substitute for hugs and cuddles. She was used to visiting them at least three times a year, and the girls spent two weeks with her every summer. Sometimes, the computer visits hurt almost more than not seeing them at all.

But the hardest part of the whole pandemic was the feeling of being on an island, surrounded by people who just didn't care, people who did nothing to help stop the spread of the virus. They crowded into bars and onto beaches and they gallivanted through the country when they didn't need to, and worst of all, they refused to even wear a mask. Such carelessness was beyond her comprehension. She desperately wanted to see her grandchildren, and it wasn't safe to travel. Some days, she felt that she'd never see them again because people wouldn't take even the most basic precautions for the good of the whole of society.

Nancy poured a cup of coffee and went to the refrigerator for milk. When she pulled the cap off, it smelled even worse than she did. Darn. Nancy ordered her groceries online and they loaded them in her car, curbside. She forgot to get milk yesterday. The minimum order for pickup was fifty dollars, so she couldn't afford to get more groceries until next week.

She watched tears splash into her coffee, swirling on the surface for a moment before getting sucked under and disappearing into the darkness. One more way the pandemic was upending her life. She cried for a few minutes and blew her nose. Maybe she could drink her coffee black, just for a few days. She sipped and shuddered.

She loved coffee with milk and looked forward to it every morning. It was one of the few pleasures she maintained throughout the pandemic, and she didn't want to give it up, not even for a week. Nancy considered. Last month, the governor issued a mask mandate. She could be in and out of the convenience store in five minutes and everyone would be wearing masks, so it should be safe enough. She wanted that milk. Glaring at her cup, Nancy made a daring decision. She marched into the bathroom, showered, put on clean clothes, brushed her teeth, grabbed her keys, and opened the kitchen door to the garage. She stopped for a moment, gathering her courage, then got into her car.

When she arrived at the store, she parked at the edge of the lot, shoved her wallet in her pocket, and kept her head down as she walked inside. Her joints complained as she pulled open the door, a constant reminder of why she needed to be extra careful. She was almost to the refrigerator section when she noticed three bare-faced people at the checkout. She glanced around; only about half the people in the store had face coverings. What the heck? She thought about leaving, but she was here now, and she really wanted that milk. Damn them all. What was their problem?

Nancy saw the uniformed deputy at the refrigerator case. He was probably ten years younger than her son, with cherub cheeks and a buzz cut that gave him a sweet, almost vulnerable, appearance. He was eyeing the soft drinks, and he wasn't wearing a mask. She was horrified. He was an officer of the law, someone who should be setting an example.

Nancy couldn't stop herself. "Why aren't you wearing a mask?"

He glanced at her and turned back to the drink selection, grimacing. "Sorry, I left it in my car. I was just going to grab a soda and go."

Thinking that he should have gone back to his car for the mask, Nancy was glad he, at least, had the decency to look embarrassed. She reached for the refrigerator handle when a woman with a headband and ponytail bumped her shoulder. "Don't worry about the masks. They don't do any good anyway. I never wear one."

Nancy stepped back quickly, appalled about being touched by this stranger. She was surrounded by recklessness. Nancy glared, but didn't respond. No one seemed to even consider maintaining a six-foot social distance. She noticed the middle-aged woman's workout clothes and wondered if she was on her way to the gym.

A young man, dressed in jeans and a dark green T-shirt adorned with the angriest eagle Nancy had ever seen, joined the conversation. "You've got that right. I'm not going to be forced to live in fear and have my rights and freedom taken away."

What about my rights and freedom? Nancy wanted to scream, but instead she backed up again and spoke quietly, "There's an order from the governor. Masks are required."

Eagle-shirt guy shrugged. "Don't you watch the news? The county sheriffs in Wisconsin are too fucking busy to bother chasing after people about something as stupid as a mask. I bet it's not even legal."

Then he grinned, and she could visualize the virus dripping off his teeth. Grainy gray droplets flying through the air, unrestrained by cotton or common sense, heading straight for her already compromised lungs. At that moment, staring at his lips, curled in the definition of smug, something deep inside of her snapped. She'd stayed home for months and she was going to have to stay home for many more and she was lonely and scared and missing her family and these people couldn't be bothered to comply with a simple mandate because their rights were so damn important. More important than hers, apparently.

Trying to regain control, she turned away from the man and took a shallow breath. The sign on the front door caught her attention and suddenly lit up, shimmering pink and green neon. "No Shirt, No Shoes, No Service" flashed over and over, almost blinding her with its intensity. Nancy swiveled and glared at the maskless strangers. "Fine, I understand rights. I have them, too. Why should I follow the rules if you don't? I've always hated shoes. I never had to wear shoes in stores when I was young. Then they made those stupid health laws, and all of a sudden, I have to wear shoes everywhere I go. Well, they cramp my feet. My toes have a right to be free." She stepped out of her Crocs and kicked them across the floor, slowly, one at a time.

The man and woman laughed. Out of the corner of her eye, Nancy saw the deputy set his soda bottle beside the newspapers and walk toward them from the checkout line.

"Ma'am, please put your shoes back on."

"No." Her scream was muffled by the fabric covering her mouth. "Shoes make it impossible for my feet to breathe. I'm not a sheep. It's my right to go without shoes and shirts and you can't deny me service." She continued to glare, bored her eyes into his, just daring him to do something as she grabbed the bottom of her light-blue 2009 Folk Festival T-shirt and lifted it slowly over her head.

"Ma'am. Leave your clothes on, please." The officer's voice was almost pleading.

Nancy felt a bit sorry for him, but she was beyond caring. "Go ahead, make my day." She twirled the T-shirt around her head like a lariat and let it fly in a perfect trajectory to hit workout gal smack in the face.

The pony-tailed woman grabbed Nancy's shirt and flung it to the floor. "You crazy old bitch."

"You bet I am." For the first time in her life, Nancy felt proud to be called a bitch.

The deputy made a grab for her, but Nancy backed up, amazed at her own quick reflexes. She was beyond thinking now, acting purely on instinct.

She unhooked her bra, letting her breasts fly free. She felt them swing as she jumped sideways and smashed into a wire rack holding a display of potato chips. That startled her and she stopped long enough for the officer to grab her arm.

"Ma'am, please. I'm going to have to take you in."

"Nooooo." She was not going. She kicked at him but missed and hit the counter. Her big toe felt like it cracked in two and she crumpled to the ground, wrenching free from his grasp and landing on scattered yellow bags of snacks. As she went down, she counted four people holding up cell phones.

"Goddammit, lady." He helped her up, pulled her arms behind her, and encircled her wrists in metal cuffs.

"Ow, ow, ow, ow," Nancy kept screaming. She could tell he was trying to be gentle, but her arthritic joints were blazing.

"I'm sorry." He guided her to the parking lot and helped her into the police car. "I have protocols I have to follow." He shut the door and went back into the store.

As she sat there, shoeless and naked from the waist up, the enormity of her situation sunk in. She'd been so careful for all these months, and now, because she had to have milk for her coffee, maskless people spewed germs in her face and this young officer manhandled her. These people were exposed all day long to God knows who. Now he was taking her to jail where she'd be put in a cell with dozens of others who probably weren't wearing masks either. That thought truly frightened her. She started to shake.

Laughter outside the car caught her attention and she realized people were staring. Of course, they were staring. She was a crazy old woman with wispy gray hair that hadn't seen a stylist in six months and wrinkly, drooping breasts. She just did a striptease in a Quik Mart and attacked a cop. She didn't even know who she was at this point.

Nancy's hands were still cuffed behind her, so she couldn't do anything to hide either her breasts or her shame. On top of all that, the car smelled moldy. She sneezed three times and her nose started running, dampening the inside of her mask. What was she thinking? This wasn't like her. None of this was like her at all. She had lived a mostly conventional, ordinary, even boring life. This was so out of character, she almost laughed. Then without warning, she felt the heat of humiliation cover her, and she just wanted to go home. Where was that cop?

As if reading her mind, he opened the door, and Nancy jumped. His eyes averted, he laid her shirt over her breasts, put her bra beside her on the seat, her shoes on the floor, asked for her name and address, and shut the door again. She saw him leaning against the car, talking on his phone and heard snatches of words. "Old woman," "crying," "crowds, cameras." She felt sorry for him, poor guy; it was probably a bit traumatic, like accidentally seeing his grandmother naked.

He got into the front seat and, without a word, started the car and drove away.

"Where are you taking me?" Her voice quivered.

"We're going to the police station. It's just a couple miles." About ten minutes later, he pulled into an underground garage, put the car in park, got out, and opened the back door.

"I talked to my sergeant." The officer stared at a point just over her head. "He said that since you don't have any record, and if you're willing to apologize, we could just let this whole thing go. Those people in the store provoked you. We can call it a mistake. No one got hurt, after all. What do you say?"

"Apologize?" Nancy said. "To whom? To you?"

Red streaked the man's neck, and again, Nancy thought this must be embarrassing for him. He was so very young. "Well, no, you don't really have to apologize so much as promise that you won't do anything like this again."

Nancy stared at him while she considered. They were giving her a way out, and she should embrace it. She certainly didn't want to go to jail. She thought about taking a stand, getting arrested, using this opportunity to tell her side of the story, and maybe to convince people of the importance of masks in the middle of a pandemic, but she couldn't. She was tired and scared and her foot hurt. Her outrage was all used up. She just wanted to go home and hope any video floating out there would be drowned in the sea of short attention spans.

She sighed. "I'm sorry for the trouble I caused. I promise I won't ever do it again." Her voice, stifled by her mask, sounded forlorn. He uncuffed her hands and turned his back as she got dressed. Then he took her to the convenience store. No crowd lingered, so she slipped into her car unnoticed and drove home, carefully keeping two miles below the posted speed limit.

Safely back in her kitchen, still without unspoiled milk, Nancy made a fresh pot of her favorite blend. Her head was pounding, and she thought caffeine might help. She tasted the black coffee and grimaced. Too bitter.

Her phone chimed with a text from an old friend.

"Is this you?"

Nancy clicked the link and was immediately back in the store, raging. She realized her hope that this incident would somehow go unnoticed was fruitless. Oh my god. She played the video three times, amazed that the person she was watching was actually her.

Nancy wanted to turn off her phone and go back to bed. She didn't have the strength to deal with this. Would she ever be able to explain why she stripped half-naked in public and tried to kick a police officer? God, what would Max say? Hopefully, he could keep it from the girls. Or maybe it would just stay local.

Nancy hit reply, confirmed the video was indeed her, and she would call later to explain. She drank more coffee and sighed at the taste. Her landline rang in the living room, startling her, but old habits kicked in and she answered without thinking.

"Mrs. Gifford?"

"Yes?"

"This is Renata Simmons. I'm a reporter for the *Winston Gazette*. I'd like to talk to you about the events you were involved in at Quik Mart this morning."

Nancy's fingers tightened on the receiver. Her first instinct was to slam it down, but the reporter kept talking so, raised to be polite, she kept listening.

"I saw the video of your altercation. I thought maybe you'd like to tell our readers your version of the experience."

Nancy pursed her lips. Did she want to tell her side? Did she want to explain why her frustration and anger boiled over and swept her away? She remembered her conversation with the officer, her desire to take a stand. Now was her chance. But did she really want to put herself so far out there, be in the public eye? Was it better to just let this die?

"One minute please." She set the receiver down and swallowed a bit more of her coffee. It was cooler now, and strangely, less unpleasant. She drank again. Maybe she could get used to drinking it without milk after all. She took a third sip while she thought about the last six months, her loneliness, depression, and despair over what she believed was an incredible lack of empathy. She thought of her granddaughters and what she wanted for them and their future. Right or wrong, her actions had presented her with an opportunity. She was going to take advantage of it.

A voice on the phone reminded her the reporter was still waiting.

"Ma'am, are you there?"

She nodded, then picked up the receiver and spoke. "Yes, I'm here."

"I just have a few questions."

Nancy settled herself comfortably on the couch and drank more coffee. "Go ahead."

Poetry | *Christine Rhein*

MASKED

———

May 2020

In the checkout line at Kroger,
    the woman, six feet or so
ahead, is talking through her mask,
    its flowery fabric,
telling me about the weather—
    the frost, surely gone,
and the nursery in town, open now,
    how it's safe to shop there
early, before everyone else.
    I wonder if, somehow,
I know her by her eyes and hair,
    or if it's just the way
she's nodding, letting me go on
    about that guy
without a mask, back in the aisles,
    showing off his face,
his smirk, hardly buying anything,
    but touching, touching,
touching. She says she saw him too,
    then stops to look around—
customers to the right, the left—
    before saying she wanted
to smack him. It's hard to keep up,
    she says—her daughter

and son, home from college,
    eating like they're still
on a meal plan, and her husband
    coming home hungry
from long shifts at his hospital
    in Detroit. I try to nod—
not too much, nor too little—
    and to tell her how pretty
her mask is, to ask if she sewed
    it herself, but no time
now, both of us needing to push
    our carts forward,
for her to unload. I can't help
    but see—eggs, milk,
bananas, potatoes—how she
    stacks as fast as she can,
races against the conveyer,
    everyone racing, alone.

MELT DOWN

———

Two hundred million face masks
are produced each day in China.
Demand grows daily yet numbers
still fail our world's great need.
Mask makers melt plastic into
airy ribbons of fabric that resemble
cotton candy. Gossamer wings
afloat along the Milky Way.
Blown glass turns to filigree.
Each strand will transform lives.

Dirt floors, frozen pipes, rusted gears,
upturned tables must be transformed
like fairy tales to state-of-art assembly
lines. Former shoe factories, iPhone
plants, diaper mills retooled for camouflage.
Supervisors dispense mops, brooms,
wrenches, oil cans as if they were
military armaments. Workers
line streets to enlist. Hours are long.
Pay is short. Orders unquestioned.

As desperation overwhelms supply,
sweatshops grow worldwide. Locked in
as fibers melt, spin, blow and blend,
many are too young to recall Rana
Plaza's collapse into flames, its

smoke-streaked bodies mingled with striped
shirt fabric and denim jackets,
as weeping families raged against
shadows. Marketplace amnesia.
We need these goods. Scrutiny melts away.

MAY 6, 2020

---

the noise

was military.
Blue Angel

or Thunder-

bird?
supposed

to honor

health-
care

workers.

an expensive
700 mile

per hour

fore-
boding fly-

over. over

the jobless.
the isolated.

the sick.

even
the ones

who won't

cover or be
masked.

BARRIERS

———

(*4/7/2020*)

The homeless man, whom I'll call Gerald, hunched on the end of my exam table, gingerly picking at the metal shield taped over his left eye. "It happened like this, see, I was out panhandling, and with this new virus thing I've been trying to keep to myself, so I moved down the block from my usual spot. I'm standing there with my sign and my can for maybe five minutes, and a guy I've never seen before comes up, says I'm in his space. Before I can say anything, he lands a shot, right here. I think he was wearing a heavy ring or something, because I feel a pop and a squelch, and blood starts pouring from my eye socket, and right away I know my sight is done." He sighed. "I was trying to do the right thing, stay apart from people as much as possible, you know? Because of that I lose my eye."

I lean forward and sigh, too, trying to express as much concern as I can with just my eyes above the line of my mask.

———

The *Oxford English Dictionary* lists a number of definitions for the word "mask," beginning with this:

—from the French *masque*: a covering for the face, and related senses.

———

Here we are in this pandemic, covering our faces to protect ourselves and each other from a virus, while at the same time uncovering newly raw emotions we sense in one another: fear, grief, bewilderment, empathy. The mask is a barrier to keep us safe; how to keep it from being a barrier to our humanity?

————

—A covering for the mouth and nose made of fiber or gauze, designed to filter dust, microorganisms, etc., from air inhaled or exhaled, esp. by theatre staff during surgical operations.

————

I'm a nurse practitioner, and I've been working with people caught in homelessness at Boston Health Care for the Homeless Program (BHCHP) for twenty years. I'm astonished at the speed with which my clinical world has been transformed since mid-March, as the program geared up for a wave of COVID infections to sweep through our vulnerable homeless community. BHCHP administrators and clinicians worked around the clock with city and state agencies to set up a new tent-based testing center in a parking lot next to our main building and to procure unused blocks of rooms in nearby college dormitories and hotels to house people needing to be quarantined.

I recently turned sixty, and Health Care for the Homeless management has determined that older clinicians like me, who are at higher risk for serious complications from COVID-19, won't be working as frontline caregivers in this unfolding crisis. So I've been part of the support team, caring for our "regular" patients recovering from hip surgery or receiving breast cancer treatment, freeing up younger clinicians to prepare for the storm of COVID infections. In the early days of the crisis, when institutions were frantically scrambling to stock personal protective equipment, those of us who were seeing non-COVID patients were mostly mask-less as we went about our work, wearing gloves only for procedures. I washed my hands thirty-plus times a shift: between each patient, every time I pulled a door handle or moved an equipment cart—or at least I tried to. I talked to patients from a respectful distance, laying hands on them or listening to their heart and lungs only if really necessary, scrubbing down my stethoscope afterward with antiseptic wipes. It was exhausting to maintain a hyperawareness of every surface that I touched, of the safe distances I needed to keep between myself and others as I moved around the clinic.

Starting on Monday, March 31, all clinical staff were issued one surgical mask each to wear for the entire shift. At that time, at that rate of use, our program had on hand a sixteen-day supply of masks for the two hundred or so essential on-site staff members. Since then, we've procured more surgical masks, and more protective equipment for our frontline clinicians: gowns and face shields and the more secure N95 masks. But on that day, I appreciated how precious a thirty-five-cent pleated surgical mask can be. The sheer close physical presence of this thing on my face, molded over the bridge of my nose and the swell of my cheekbones, helped me to remember in each moment that we were moving into a deepening health care crisis. I was aware of each breath circulating through the narrow space between my skin and fabric, growing sweetly stale by shift's end. The crinkly fabric was a physical reminder that I couldn't touch my face, something I realized I did compulsively when I was mask-less. I kept the mask in place except for a quick lunch break, when I carefully removed it by the ear loops and placed it, outside fabric facedown, on a clean sheet of paper on my desk beside me while I inhaled my food, then picking it up again only by the ear loops, to set it back over my face, followed by yet another thorough twenty-second handwashing.

———

—A grotesque or comical representation of a face, made of pasteboard, plastic, or other material, and worn at carnivals, parties, etc.

———

It's only been a couple of months, but it seems like a decade since I attended the sprawling AWP (Association of Writers and Writing Programs) convention in San Antonio at the beginning of March. Early reports of clusters of US citizens coming down with a deadly novel coronavirus, on cruise ships and in West Coast nursing homes, were just beginning to emerge in the weeks leading up to the convention, and organizers chose to go ahead with the conference. About a quarter of the anticipated twelve thousand participants made last-minute decisions not to attend. I opted to go, and although I was disappointed by the scores of canceled readings and panels, and the many absent editors and literary figures I'd hoped to meet, I did have a pleasant time strolling along the Riverwalk, meeting up with far-flung writerly friends, sitting outside in the soft Texas spring air while nursing margaritas and trading stories. The cavernous convention center seemed both eerily empty and strangely intimate, as we didn't have to fight our way through tight throngs of high-strung literati to find our way around. Most everyone adhered to the brand-new social distancing guidelines: no handshakes or hugs, but elbow bumps were okay. The sour pungency of hand sanitizer wafted through the convention center halls, as organizers had placed Purell dispensers every twenty yards or so.

At the end of the four-day convention, my friend Rex gave me a cloth face mask with a goofy cartoon smiley-mouth stenciled on it to wear in the confines of the air cabin on my flight home. I accepted it as a joke gift, and stuck it in my pocket, not realizing how soon it would become a required accessory for routine activities: grocery shopping, walking the dogs around the neighborhood. How quickly our social norms have changed.

———

—A facial expression assumed deliberately to conceal an emotion or give a false impression; an outward appearance which belies a person's true nature.

———

Of course, we've all been on edge, hunkering down in our homes, wondering what comes next for the world in this moment of climbing infection rates, plunging employment, and gyrating economic markets. I tell myself I'm fine, and on the surface it's true: my wife and I both have secure jobs for now; we have a roof over our heads, and a well-stocked pantry. Most everyone I know, my family and friends, are healthy and secure at this point. The people I know who have succumbed to COVID-19 are not part of my immediate life: distant relatives of friends; my high school math teacher. So I put on a calm demeanor and focus on getting through each day, looking to the immediate tasks at hand, avoiding unnecessary drama. But each night I wake up in the predawn and lie there for an hour or so, wondering. I'm not paralyzed with dread, but I'm not calm, either.

Early in April, I received a call from my medical director. He informed me I had an exposure, that one of the patients I saw the previous week had tested positive for COVID-19. He said that it was likely not a significant exposure, as I was following our clinical care protocols, and I was wearing a mask, but that I should be scrupulous about social distancing for the remainder of the fourteen days after the exposure, and if I had any symptoms—fever, dry cough, or severe fatigue—that I should come in and get tested.

After I hung up the phone, I realized this was not surprising news; I'd been expecting such a call at some point. I told my wife, and we rationally ticked through the household changes we'd already been thinking we might have to make at some point: I would move out of the bedroom and sleep on the sofa in the study; I would cease involvement in food prep; I would steer clear of our two teen girls as much as possible, shower in the downstairs bathroom, take my temperature every morning. I looked out the window. It was a beautiful spring day, the forsythia was blooming out back, and I felt fine. But the "what-ifs" hung in the air: what if at some point I didn't feel fine, or Anna, or both of us, or all of us? What then? I took a breath, slipped on my calm demeanor, washed my hands again, and set about moving my clothes and toiletries into the study.

———

—A likeness of a person's face in clay, wax, etc., *esp.* one made by taking a mold from the face itself.

———

From the late Middle Ages up into the twentieth century a death mask, cast from wax or plaster that had been molded directly to the newly deceased person's face, was a significant form of commemoration for kings and nobility and other eminent persons. Such renowned figures as Dante Alighieri, Henry VIII, Beethoven, Voltaire, John Keats, and Stalin all had death masks taken and cast, so that their features would be permanently fixed, to be remembered by successive generations. In the nineteenth century, death masks were sometimes cast from unidentified bodies so that family members might be able to identify them later on. Now, ICU nurses hold up iPhones to dying COVID patients so their families, sequestered at home, can glimpse them one last time. I think of these families, with so little to carry forward with them, no last words or touch to commemorate the loved one they lost so suddenly to this virus. And I think of them cooped up in their separate homes, unable to come together to grieve their loss as a community. I think of my homeless patient, Hugh, who once told me his biggest fear was dying alone. "It can get crazy out there, Rob, but in the end, we all look out for each other. Nobody, I tell you, nobody wants to die alone."

One night, I took the dogs out for a late loop around the block. The full moon was luminous, mostly hidden behind clouds. Beyond a line of trees across the street, spring peepers were chiming at full volume, a joyous chorus of frogs seeking mates as they carried their life cycle into another season of renewal. For a moment, the world was so achingly beautiful that it masked the human suffering and loss I knew was unfolding farther out there in the night. Suffering and beauty. I had no idea which side of the barrier I might be standing on.

Previously published in *Scoundrel Time*

Poetry | *Stephanie Lenox*

FROM *THE QUARANTINAS*

––––––––

i zhë anwé
(just fine/in spite of everything)[1]

Even when I'm not OK, I'm OK. As in *oll korrect*, satirical misspelling that confounds spellcheck. The word's exact origin is unknown—too many false etymologies have tangled in that family tree. Like me. I'm OK. I'm *i zhë anwé*.

You Know Things Are Bad
When This Introvert Is Out

My face mask is a parachute that catches my breath as we make our way around the capitol building in a city named for peace. How is it possible my heart can continue to break into smaller and smaller pieces?

Attending a Funeral from my Living Room[2]

No one looks like themselves, not Grandpa in his flag-festooned casket, not my cousin driving to her mother's house with her infant in back, not my aunts and uncles, brother and sister, all in boxes together on a black screen.

––––––––

1   *i zhë anwé* (pronounced ee JUH on-way) is a Bodwéwadmimwen phrase, the language of my tribe.
2   In memory of Ralph J. Wilson (1930–2020), storyteller, tribal elder, veteran, who passed away on November 11 from complications resulting from the coronavirus

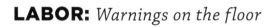

LABOR: *Warnings on the floor*

"A COVID RELIEF. FOOD FOR HOMELESS," PHOTOGRAPH
TOM DARIN LISKEY, 2020

BEZOS KNOWS

———

just like those senators
dumped
airline stock

two-dollar raise, VET (that's voluntary

extra time for you non-amazombies),
then mandatory, but backed off

that, taped warnings on the floor
so we'd keep three feet
apart

  at the time clocks
where we used to gather
    bunched hundreds
but there's been a staggering

        of the shifts

and they won't punish us anymore
if we stay home sick   right now
and they say we will get paid
if we can prove   we have COVID-19

but there are no tests for us and I don't know about the rest
           but I sure as shit can't afford
        a grand deductible doctor

two bucks more 'til April's end
double time now
on any day off   we come in

maybe he knows it'll be that long
like those, one of those, who knows
maybe just waiting to see
how many of us drop
into a mass casualty   makeshift
soccer field
to reassess
numbers

Essay | *Maya Lear Brewer*

WE ARE FAMILY: A LESSON LEARNED AS AN ONLINE ENGLISH TEACHER DURING COVID-19

The clock counts down. At the ten-second mark, I press the start button. The lesson arrives on the screen. Today's lesson: "An American visits China." I hear the giggles, and the "heart" button ping as an eager student anticipates their teacher. Through technology that dumbfounds me, these precious faces from China greet me each morning. Their love for learning and dedication is a teacher's high—an adrenaline rush expressed with my bright, wide-open eyes and cheek-aching smiles.

I've often described this teaching format as a live, interactive children's show for English-language learners. My facial expressions and hand motions are exaggerated; my speech is simple and slowly paced; my green grunting pig (a toy stolen from my dog) is a "surprise" prop for many lessons. I often laugh with them as they laugh at me singing off-key to coax them to speak new vocabulary words or to read sentences. I know this is a job, but it's so much more. This job connects me with my own lost Dutch-Indonesian heritage. As I teach these children, my heart fills, almost explodes with joy. Though we cannot speak each other's native tongue, love teleports through a screen one twenty-five minute class at a time.

Sadly, the cultural connections I've had with China are the things my immigrant mom and grandparents have brought from the Far East. As a first generation American on my mother's side, I didn't give much thought to that blue-and-white porcelain tea set inherited from my grandparents, nor my love for Asian cuisine. The heirloom, though beautiful, is rarely used. The delicious Chinese food is devoured. My menagerie of "Made in China" products fills my closets, countertops, and cabinets. The products were all priced right, and their quality is good

99

enough. But none of these things meant I knew about my own distinct culture, or valued these items, or the place and people from which they originated. It was simply and shamefully my consumerism. This was my American life, until it shifted.

Everything changed for me three years ago when I started teaching for an online company in Beijing. Now China impacts me daily. It's what gets me up most mornings. I'm not a morning person, but somehow in my groggy stupor I amble out of bed between five and six, slip on my orange T-shirt and faded black stretchy pants, and drag a brush through my hair before heading downstairs to grab a cup of coffee. Then I sit in stillness for twenty minutes to pray, write, and review lessons before I apply my fuchsia lipstick and awaken the computer.

Every morning, each one-on-one encounter with my students has also awakened me. My life has become richer as we "sit" in each other's homes, not over a meal, but over English. I've been introduced to siblings, parents, and grandparents. And I, too, have become a student, as they have taught me small Chinese phrases, culture, and the latest Chinese pop star bands. I've met beautiful, studious, and energetic children, aged three to sixteen years old. I am known as "Teacher Maya" to over 275 students of the company's 2020 current record of five hundred thousand students.

Just this morning as I sat talking with Jerry, teasing him into reading "Forbidden City" for his "An American Visits China" lesson, I thought about how two summers ago, my husband, son, daughter, and I taught in two English immersion camps for nineteen days in Beijing. On that occasion, Jerry and his mother took a four-hour high-speed train ride from Shanghai to Beijing to meet "Teacher Maya." I was overwhelmed by their generosity of spending three days away from home to be with us, and for paying for our family's lunch and dinner expenses, making sure we dined at authentic regional restaurants. And here, on the screen before us, we were looking at this familiar landmark.

"Jerry, what is it?" I say as I circle the image on the screen. Jerry offers the Chinese name. "English, Jerry, English." He places his hand on the top of his head and crinkles his nose. "I don't know," he says.

He pauses, and adds, "We go with teacher family." Suddenly he turns the screen to his left. On the wall is a photo of Jerry, his mom, and our family against the red and golden staircase within the Forbidden City. We're on his wall. I'm on his wall.

A smile stretches across Jerry's face. His two front teeth have grown in since that visit. What a privilege it had been to meet Jerry face to face, hug to hug, tickle to tickle. The love exuded through the screen and over time had proved true for both families. But not only for Jerry's, but also for other students who would come to meet us on that trip, like Ian, Max, and Zoe.

———

Only a few months ago, I was riveted as I watched the coronavirus begin to dot China's landscape. Before the rest of the world was paying attention, the earliest news came through my Facebook teaching groups. The articles from the *China Daily* said a few cases of an unidentifiable flu-like virus had appeared in Wuhan. Later, a strange story about a woman eating a bat, a Wuhan delicacy, began repeating on my Twitter feed.

Within a couple of weeks, "corona" swallowed the whole city of Wuhan while beer memes saturated Twitter. I scoured broader news sources for scraps, but it was mostly speculative of how the first few people contracted the virus, a diseased bat, a dirty meat market, and eventually, a Wuhan lab. From our earliest news it seemed isolated to the Wuhan province. The Chinese government locked down the city. The coronavirus didn't seem like much of anything.

At the time, three of my family members and a friend were planning to teach English at a winter camp for three weeks during the Chinese New Year. After having taught for two consecutive summers in Beijing, Hainan Island, also called the "Hawaii of China," was a welcome adventure. However, when the camp dates were rearranged, our family postponed the trip until summer. Our friend continued the journey without us, landing in China on January 12, only to be evacuated before the winter camp would even begin. He managed to leave China before the virus moved to Hainan Island, and was promptly quarantined once he arrived home. Before leaving China, our friend contacted us with the news that we wouldn't be going back this summer.

In our conversations, we never believed the virus, now known as COVID-19, would come to our country. Our family sighed with relief at our near miss. We had been spared. However, a looming concern overwhelmed me for those I know and love in China, for their nation, and for the children I'd see daily on my screen.

I studied the China map as it changed from yellow to red as virus cases and deaths swelled. I watched videos showing the abandoned streets of Beijing, where my family and I had once traveled, now filled with eerie silence. Beijing never sleeps. The empty streets were haunting and death-like. I was sobered. What was happening in this land so far away?

When I saw the videos of the Chinese singing anthems and calling to each other from their skyscraper apartment windows my heart was moved by their solidarity. "Stay Strong Wuhan! Stay Strong China!" I prayed and reposted on my social media accounts. I wanted the world to know this was happening to my friends, my students, their families.

In other videos brave nationals spoke of the number of deaths, of no testing, of leaving the old to die, and of how people were trapped and misplaced because of holiday travels. I saw pictures of exhausted doctors and nurses hidden in hazmat suits sleeping on hospital floors. My mind drifted to one of my summer camp students, Raine. His father was the lead doctor at the brand-new hospital we toured last summer in Beijing. Was it now overwhelmed with frightened patients? Was Raine's dad sleeping on the floor in a hazmat suit unable to go home to be with his family? So many images, so many memories, so many unknowns—my heart ached—I cried.

Then I saw reports of the mask shortage. China needed masks. A group of online teachers banded together to send them. Only a few of the company's sixty thousand teachers were able to purchase and send masks. I was one of those who tried to send masks. My local stores were sold out and future shipments delayed. The online prices were inflated. A set of fifty masks was $250. The shipping costs were an additional

$270. I didn't have the money. I felt powerless, useless to offer assistance. By day, I continued searching the internet for options. By night, I lost sleep. In the end, teachers discovered only a small percentage of students' families received the masks.

As the days passed, my job, my connection with these families, became more valuable. Many of my students still met me each morning, sometimes in tears for a lost loved one, or in fear of getting the virus, or with intense boredom from being confined for weeks. Some of my students haven't been in my classroom for the last few months. Perhaps it's because of scheduling issues, but I may never know. Through this pandemic, I have worried and prayed for them. I've told them to stay strong—my heart is with them. I've asked through WeChat—"Are you okay?" They responded, "We are keeping strong. Please pray."

In the news reports, the China map changed to red—every part infected; then North and South Korea, Hong Kong. A few more dots showed in other parts of the world. Then the cloud of red moved to Italy, France, the UK, America. The world is now a different color on all the maps.

———

On April 6 when I saw Jerry's cheerful face he didn't know I needed him—his smile, his joy, his hope, his innocence. He didn't know my ninety-six-year-old mother-in-law, who lives in a retirement home in our neighborhood, had tested positive for the virus. He didn't know our family stood outside her window to tell her we loved her the day before. She couldn't hear us. But as she lay weak in bed, she raised her frail hand to wave at us.

We didn't know if that moment would be the last time we'd see her, or if she'd have to be rushed to the hospital to die all by herself. That morning I awoke with a sad, fearful, and uncertain heart. Seeing Jerry, half a world away, lifted me, if only for a moment, reminding me beauty and laughter can live with sadness, uncertainty, and fear.

The next day, Ian's dad came on the screen and told me he was sending me masks. I wasn't sure if we'd ever receive them. In record time, nine blue surgical masks arrived. I thanked him through WeChat. He responded, "You are welcome—we are family." A tiny red emoji heart ended the text. I pondered this. "We are family."

On April 19, my mother-in-law died of COVID-19. She didn't have the "classic" symptoms. The virus took away her desire to eat, to drink, to speak, to engage in life. The gift of her last words to us were "I love you" before silence engulfed her as she drifted away. We received the phone call that Sunday evening. She'd gone to heaven.

The next morning, I didn't want to leave my bed. I hadn't canceled my classes. Somehow, I poured myself into my classes. Ian's mom came on the screen at the end of my last class for the day. "Are you okay?" she asked. She must have sensed I was teaching with a broken heart behind my smile. "My mother-in-law, my husband's mother, died last night. She got COVID-19. She's gone." I stopped myself from crying. She held her hand to her heart.

After I pressed the exit button, I texted them to clarify the details. Ian's father responded: "Hearing this news, my family and I are very sad. I hope your mother-in-law can rest in peace. COVID is temporary, and life will continue. Everyone is under incomparable pressure. I hope you and your family (are) healthy and everything is okay." Praying hands and hugging emojis followed. Tears landed on my phone screen.

To think a few months ago when all this started in China, my heart ached for them. I felt powerless to change anything. All I could do was to pray and cheer them on—bringing hope and love through a video screen. I am learning that indeed we are family—extended all across the world—even more so now as we fight for life, for health, for keeping one another safe. By offering our small gifts—space, masks, toilet paper, Zoom visits, groceries, or even English—it translates to hope. We must keep the hope alive for each other.

Poetry | *Ben Gunsberg*

LINE SPEED

————

for Hugo Dominguez

Three weeks after Trump's executive order—
Keep meat plants open!—you cut
flesh shoulder to shoulder because
closures = shortages = higher prices.

To keep meat plants open, you cut
plastic, screen space, dream shelter.
Closure = shortage = higher prices =
no protection. Spittle splatters

plastic screens. For shelter, some
raise walls between each station.
Protection? Spittle splatters when
one sneezes, coughs. Dread

rises within each station.
You receive unpaid leave if absent,
so you snuff sneeze, hush cough.
Line speeds slow if sick stay home.

You receive unpaid leave if absent = $0
= 0 sausage = hunger < profit.
Line speeds slow if sick stay home.
Plants remain open because no pork

= 0 sausage = 0 profit = shareholder
hunger. Meat rots when plants shutter.
Doors must remain open or else
reductions in beef, pork, chicken.

Some line up when plants reopen, wait,
shoulder to shoulder, box flesh.
"Quality Sausage killed him," friends say,
six weeks after Trump's executive order.

Essay | *C. Liegh McInnis*

STAYING SOCIALLY AND POLITICALLY ACTIVE WHILE SOCIALLY DISTANCING: MAKING THE ISSUES AROUND COVID-19 PART OF ONE'S ACTIVISM

———

It is important to remember that we can still be socio-politically engaging even while social distancing. Longtime Mississippi community and grassroots organizer Mac Epps emailed me on April 18, 2020, about the struggles of his mother and so many poor folks of color during this pandemic. While we all appreciate Tyson Foods donating chicken to various organizations, Epps reminds us to remain diligent in addressing how factories, such as Tyson, PECO, and Sanderson Farms, continue to maintain inhumane working conditions and treatment of its employees. Moreover, Governor Tate Reeves has named Sanderson Farms' CEO Joe Sanderson the chair of the Commission for Economic Recovery, which is not surprising since Sanderson, a major Republican supporter, has a horrendous record of employee treatment. Epps's mother is sixty-one and travels one hour in a van to Tyson every day. That is one hour to work and one hour from work, which shows just how limited employment is in Mississippi. She was called into the office Monday, April 6, 2020, and informed that two people with whom she rides to work tested positive for COVID-19. Tyson gave her sick leave for one week and made her return to work Tuesday, April 14, 2020, without being tested. They threatened her and the other workers who ride in that van with getting deducted a point for missing work. Moreover, Epps shares the story of a PECO worker who contracted COVID-19 under similar conditions. The PECO employee also lost his mother to COVID-19 and was still in the hospital when I received word from Epps.

Yet Epps continues that it is not just the corporate crooks who are ignoring the health and welfare of the poor, especially those of color. After being informed of being in contact with someone infected by COVID-19, Epps's mother called the COVID-19 hotline, told them her age, her condition, and that she was exposed to two people who tested positive. But she was still told that she didn't have enough symptoms to be tested. This point is important because a few, if not several, of the African Americans who died from COVID-19 were initially diagnosed with the flu, sent home, and returned to the hospital only after their symptoms became unbearable. This is an unfortunate pattern across the United States. A 2003 study, *Unequal Treatment: Confronting Racial and Ethnic Disparities in Health Care*, published by the Institute of Medicine, provides ample empirical evidence of racial and ethnic disparities in health care:

> This review yielded over 100 studies (summarized in Appendix B) that assessed racial and ethnic variation in a range of clinical procedures, including the use of diagnostic and therapeutic technologies. This body of literature, however, represents only a fraction of the published studies that investigate racial and ethnic differences in access to and use of healthcare services. Geiger (this volume), for example, has identified over 600 such articles published over the last three decades. For a more comprehensive review of this literature, the reader is referred to Geiger (this volume) or the reviews of Mayberry and colleagues (Mayberry, Mili, and Ofili, 2000), Kressin and Petersen (2001), Sheifer, Escarce and Schulman (2000), Ford and Cooper (1995), and the AMA Council on Ethical and Judicial Affairs (1990).

To be clear, *Unequal Treatment* cites over six hundred empirical-based articles published over the last thirty years that show people of color receiving substandard health care because of their race. This study, alone, justifies Epps when he writes, "I have no problem being an advocate or talking to anyone about a problem I see. My secret is I don't get angry; I STAY ANGRY at how our people are treated, at the lack of leadership, at the lack of care for our own, and because I know we can and must do better." It seems that Epps's sentiment has been proven empirically by research. Moreover, Nidhi Prakash, in her article "Doctors Are Concerned that Black Communities Might Not Be Getting Access to Coronavirus Tests," states that:

> A group of doctors in Virginia is calling for the Centers for Disease Control and Prevention and the World Health Organization to release information about whether black communities are being left behind as the shortage of coronavirus tests continues in the US. They're concerned that black communities and other underserved groups might be disproportionately missing out on getting tested for COVID-19, in the absence of data breaking down who's been tested so far by race and ethnicity.

So, in some cases, African Americans cannot gain access to testing, and in other cases, African Americans have been improperly tested only to realize later that they were infected with COVID-19. Thus, African Americans having the highest cases of COVID-19 and many other medical issues is not exclusively due to "bad choices" by Black folks. Moreover, those "bad choices" seem to be influenced, if not exasperated, by discriminatory policies and practices by the health care system. Because poor people—especially those of color—are the most at-risk group to contract COVID-19, then it would seem that policies would mandate that this group receive immediate care. However, once again, racist whites have proven that they desire to eliminate African Americans by any means necessary to maintain their reign of white supremacy, even if it means withholding medical care.

Yet now that we have been reminded of this truth, what can we do to change this issue while socially distancing, as African Americans remain disproportionately affected by COVID-19 and the health care system in general? At this point, we should be writing, calling, emailing, and texting our city, county, state, and nationally elected officials and expressing our concerns. (Of course, I'll leave the texting to y'all since I don't . . . err . . . text, but I digress.) If those fools can be outside protesting against social distancing when the data/science tells us we still need more time to flatten the curve, then rational folks can develop ways to inform our elected officials of the changes needed in health care provided to poor people, especially poor people of color. Additionally, we need to contact our elected officials and lend our voices to raise awareness regarding the substandard treatment of employees at plants like Tyson, PECO, and many others. This also means that those of us in the African American middle and upper classes must change our notions that poor people should accept whatever treatment they receive and just be happy to be employed. Often, it is middle- and upper-economic-class Black folks who refuse to come to the aid of their lower-economic brothers and sisters. Yet as the numbers continue to show, poor people and people of color need the most protection, not just from the virus, but from greedy companies like Tyson that continue to ignore the dangers and place their employees in harm's way. HuffPost reported that

> A furious Iowa sheriff blasted the "inept" and "dysfunctional" Tyson Fresh Meats plant in his county where about 900 workers contracted COVID-19. . . .
>
> [Black Hawk County Sheriff Tony Thompson said,] "We know" that the Iowa coronavirus outbreak and threats to the food supply chain are "due to these inept, reactionary and dysfunctional responses" to what was happening in the Waterloo plant, which employs 2,800 workers. . . .
>
> "It's frustrating that my citizens . . . are more at risk than any other county in the state." . . .
>
> As of Wednesday, Tyson workers were linked to about 90% of the 1,327 COVID-19 cases in Black Hawk County, which has the highest number of coronavirus in the state, USA Today reported.
>
> Additionally, about 900 of the 2,200 employees at a Tyson pork processing plant in Logansport, Indiana, have also tested positive for the coronavirus. . . . Again, that's the lion's share of the 1,200 cases in Cass County, where the plant is located (Papenfuss).

These numbers make it clear that, even during a pandemic, it is business as usual when it comes to the exploitation of the poor and people of color.

Ultimately, Epps is reminding us that evil never sleeps. In fact, evil waits for the rest of us to sleep so that it can do its evil. Just check Trump's latest executive order limiting immigration as well as the silly Mississippi attorney general Lynn Fitch preparing to file a lawsuit against China for its "cover-up" of the severity of COVID-19. Shouldn't Fitch be suing President Trump for his "cover-up" and "ineptitude," or do Fitch and all the people who voted for Trump simply consider ignorance, inaction, and ineptitude by Trump just par for the course of what it takes to maintain white supremacy? So does not the fact that Trump ignored and even dismantled President Obama's plan for a pandemic warrant suing President Agent Orange? Even Republican

> Senate Majority Leader Mitch McConnell said Thursday that he was wrong to claim former President Barack Obama didn't leave a "game plan" to deal with a pandemic when he left the White House to President Donald Trump.
>
> "I was wrong," McConnell told *Fox News'* Bret Baier. "They did leave behind a plan, so I clearly made a mistake in that regard" (Visser).

Furthermore, the *St. Louis Post-Dispatch* reports that it was Trump who had no plan and depleted the resources that President Obama had left.

> Perhaps because of his experience with the 2015 Ebola outbreak, Obama sought to leave his successor fully prepared to confront future pandemics. He asked in his fiscal 2017 budget request to boost federal isolation and quarantine funding by $15 million, to $46.6 million. Congress approved $31.6 million. In Trump's three years in office, he has not requested a dime more in funding.
>
> Obama asked to nearly double his own $40 million outlay for epidemiology and laboratory capacity. Congress balked, but Obama left Trump with that $40 million as a starting point. What did Trump do? In his 2020 budget, he asked Congress to cut that number to: Zero. Zilch. Nothing.
>
> Obama's goal was $629.5 million in funding for pandemic preparedness, though Congress only gave him $612 million. If Trump was

so worried about a bare cupboard, why did he ask Congress to cut the 2020 pandemic preparedness budget by $102.9 million? In the 2019 fiscal year budget, he sought a $595.5 million cut in the overall public health preparedness and response outlay.

The CDC budget in Obama's final year mentions "epidemiology" or derivatives of the word 252 times. Under Trump, the word appears 129 times. The phrase "pandemic preparedness" appears exactly once in Trump's 2020 budget.

Interestingly, Trump's own 2020 budget contains a chart comparing the nation's public health emergency preparedness before the Sept. 11, 2001, attacks and where it stood in 2016 (why it stops with Obama's final year is unclear). Before 9/11, the nation had a 20% ability to mobilize in response to a health emergency, a 5% ability to establish an incident-command system, and 0% storage and distribution capacity for critical medicines and supplies. By Obama's final year, the nation's preparedness on all measurements was 98% to 100%. That's by the Trump administration's own assessment. If the cupboard was bare, it's because Trump swept it clean (Editorial Board).

With this latest executive order, Trump is actually more racist and ignorant than his racist and ignorant predecessors. In 1918, during the height of the flu epidemic, America allowed more than 110,000 immigrants to enter the country. Then president Woodrow Wilson was a known racist, and during one of the greatest epidemics in American history, he did not seek to close American borders. According to Dick Lehr in "The Racist Legacy of Woodrow Wilson," "Wilson oversaw unprecedented segregation in federal offices," and when he was confronted about this in the White House by civil rights activist William Trotter, Wilson had Trotter thrown "out of the Oval Office. . . . For blacks—who ever since Lincoln's War had expected some measure of equity from the federal government—the sense of a betrayal ran deep." Interestingly enough, in a move similar to Trump, what evoked Wilson's ire was the mere fact that Trotter would even question Wilson about his segregation of federal offices, stating to Trotter, "Your tone, sir, offends me" and then had Trotter and his associates removed from the White House. It seems that we could replace Wilson's name with Trump and nothing would change. Based on this, can there be any doubt that MAGA is code for reestablishing overtly racist, sexist, and homophobic legislation? And I guess that we are never going to discuss how Canada is using less money to aid its citizens, but its citizens are receiving twice as much economic assistance as US citizens from its government? But, again, Canada decided to help its citizens rather than using a pandemic to perpetuate evil by padding the coffers of the wealthy while removing even more rights from the oppressed. As such, why don't we all unite and sue Attorney General Fitch for being an idiot? So, let's call, email, text, vote, and whatever else we can do to create policy changes that will liberate America from the evil and idiocy of those infected with the virus of white supremacy.

Works Cited

Editorial Board. "If the Pandemic-Preparedness Cupboard Was Bare, It Was Trump's Doing." *St. Louis Post-Dispatch*, May 25, 2020. https://www.stltoday.com/opinion/editorial/editorial-if-the-pandemic-preparedness-cupboard-was-bare-it-was-trumps-doing/article_bd1bb8d6-7477-590d-af72-ae4e305de601.html.

Lehr, Dick. "The Racist Legacy of Woodrow Wilson." *The Atlantic*, November 27, 2015. https://www.theatlantic.com/politics/archive/2015/11/wilson-legacy-racism/417549/. April 19, 2020.

Papenfuss, Mary. "'Incensed' Sheriff Slams 'Dysfunctional' Tyson for 900 COVID-19 Cases in Iowa Hot Spot." HuffPost, May 1, 2020. https://www.huffpost.com/entry/iowa-sheriff-tyson-plant-covid-19_n_5eab6cd3c5b62da419eed3e5.

Prakash, Nidhi. "Doctors Are Concerned That Black Communities Might Not Be Getting Access to Coronavirus Tests." BuzzFeed.com, March 22, 2020. https://www.buzzfeednews.com/article/nidhiprakash/coronavirus-tests-covid-19-black.

National Library of Medicine. *Unequal Treatment: Confronting Racial and Ethnic Disparities in Health Care*. 2003. https://www.ncbi.nlm.nih.gov/books/NBK220358/.

Visser, Nick. "McConnell Says He Was 'Wrong' to Claim Obama Didn't Leave a Pandemic Playbook." HuffPost, May 14, 2020. https://www.huffpost.com/entry/mcconnell-wrong-obama-playbook-pandemic_n_5ebded27c5b6ee0b69e82f3e.

"RETAIL WORKER," PHOTOGRAPH
TOM DARIN LISKEY, 2020

Poetry | *Michele Bombardier*

ESSENTIAL MEDICAL WORKERS
ARE TO REPORT TO DUTY

———————

My friend lives with her two children.
Predawn she rises, cooks their dinner, leaves
a note: homework, lunch, start rice
at six. They eat without her. When she gets home,
they wait at the table while she strips at the door,
puts her scrubs in the wash, retraces her steps,
bleach-wipes the doorknobs, light switch,
washer dial. She showers, then sits with them
at the kitchen table. Rice, red beans, salad.
She closes her eyes, breathes deep.
They talk in low tones. Her children are teenagers
so she answers directly when they ask
about her day at the hospital. Later,
she calls me, we pour a glass of wine
for our computer visit. When I ask if she wants
to travel after the pandemic, she shakes her head.
She asks about online legal help, updating her will,
my plans, long-term, do I want to move?
No, I say. *I'm leaving here feet first.*
I laugh at my joke but when I look at the screen,
I see her steady gaze, her slow nod.

THESE HANDS

It's not how I imagined it would go.

"Nobody cares about us construction workers," Hayes shouted down, his breath pluming in front of him. "Nobody gives a damn."

I hated arguing with Thomas Hayes, especially when he was right.

Hayes was glaring at me from the basket of his boom lift, some ten feet off the snow-and-mud-churned ground. The guy was burly, barrel-chested with a biker beard. His hard hat, worn over his winter hat, was covered in stickers—old union decals, bumper stickers, some that had seen more seasons than half the guys on this jobsite. Hayes's favorite sticker, though, stuck crooked along the left side, proclaimed that, "On the 8th Day God Created GLAZIERS!"

We were glaziers.

That's glass workers to most people. Windows and the like. Everything from houses to commercial buildings. We build and fit the frames, then install the glass. I'd worked for a few places, but Dolton Glass for the past seven years.

It's a living.

For Thomas Hayes, it's a damn *good* living.

At fifty-six, though, he was starting to lose patience, especially with general contractors like the one we were working for now. Out in the middle of nowhere, some new industrial plaza. Working on a building that would manufacture parts for washing machines.

"Clark, we shouldn't even be here," Hayes shouted, thumbing the joystick that brought the basket down. The boom lift used an electric motor, and it hummed as it worked. He waited until he was back on the ground before finishing.

I studied my boots, hoping none of the other trades on site could hear him.

Hayes unclipped his fall-arrest harness, then stepped out of the basket, his steel-toe boots crunching on the frozen ground. He patted his coat pockets, looking for his smokes. He lit one, took a long drag. "We shouldn't even be here. At all. And you're gonna give me grief for not wearing my mask. Thirty feet in the air. By myself. *Outside*."

"I know," I said. Then quieter, "I know. But it's the site rules. If the super sees—"

"The *super*? Gary's not even here, Clark. He gets to work *from home*. We're the essential workers." His tone was mocking.

I adjusted my own face mask. "I know."

"How is this essential work?"

I shrugged. "Government says."

He rolled his eyes. "Have you seen the Porta Potties here?"

I had, and he knew I had.

"You gonna tell me that's hygienic? Don't even have anywhere to wash our hands." He spat on the ground, regarding me. "Any work we do inside, any interior glass, and we're elbow to elbow with each other, with other trades. And you're worried about me wearing my mask outside on a lift?"

I was the lead hand on this job, but also fifteen years Hayes's junior. I liked to imagine that someday I would earn his respect. Today was not that day, though.

Searching for a response, I looked around the job site, considering this empty shell of a building, the skids of glass lined up along its one side for us to install. Six more weeks, maybe, and we'd be finished. Six more weeks of work. Better than some people.

So I said the only thing I could think to say. "I'm just worried about us getting paid."

Hayes spat on the ground again.

———

My wife, Debbie, has always been a worrier. She says the same thing to me every morning before I hop in the pickup and leave for work—"Be safe. I love you."

It's not just something she says.

We kiss goodbye. She squeezes my hand.

I don't give it a second thought, but she does.

Glass work can be dangerous. Hell, it can get you killed if you're unlucky or dumb enough. The problem is that glass is not only razor sharp but also heavy—not exactly a winning combination.

Sometimes, at night, as we lie in bed, Deb will reach for my hand in the dark, trace the scars there with her fingers, as if she's trying to read the stories behind each crooked line of dimpled skin, like a blind woman reading braille.

There are real hazards in glass work, but you learn to navigate them. Work in the trade long enough, and you'll see them a mile away. It's not complicated.

But then . . .

Well, then the pandemic happened.

Saying it like that—it just sounds melodramatic, doesn't it? Which is exactly what I thought in the early days.

"It's just the flu," I told my wife.

I remember the way she looked at me when I said that, like I was maybe dumber than she thought. She'd fixed me with a hard stare, her eyes a green so sharp I felt my skin part under her gaze.

"You be safe," she told me, finger to my chest, my heart.

And I'd nodded, feeling properly chastised.

But also like I was just humoring her. I was happy to do it. Still . . .

Then the schools closed, the day care centers, all retail. Hell, even the hardware stores shuttered. The day Deb came home and told me her work had done across-the-board layoffs was the first time I felt it, the change, that something was really different.

"Hey, I've still got my job," I said, trying to reassure her. "We'll be okay."

And I could see it, could believe it.

That's the trick, I thought. You have to imagine what you want, visualize it, picture it in your mind so clearly that there is only one way forward. Deb had taught me that. When I thought I couldn't be a somebody, she'd given me vision, pushed me to better. I was no CEO, but lead hand wasn't too shabby. It paid well.

"We'll be okay," I said again. "Don't worry about the bills. We'll be fine."

She just looked at me. "Money's not what I'm worried about." She put her purse on the counter and regarded me. "Do you need me to say it?"

She didn't.

———

A phone call at five in the morning, Monday, maybe a month later.

I was already up, but barely, rubbing the sleep from my eyes as I let the dog out. It was the head office.

Our job site had been shut down—an outbreak on site. I bet the super, Gary, was throwing a fit over having to close up shop. There was still more than two weeks of glass work left, never mind what other trades had left to do.

To be honest, the news came as a surprise.

I'd heard of a few other sites shutting down over the past month, but not many; I always figured we'd be fine. Naive, I know. My main worry at that point was having to give the guys the bad news.

But then one of them called me first, just as I was about to pull out of the driveway.

It was Thomas Hayes—word travels fast.

I threw the truck in park, letting it idle, my headlights casting frozen shadows across the side of my neighbor's house. The sun would rise soon; maybe the temperature would too. The heater was cranked high, so I dialed it down to hear better.

Hayes sounded terrible. Sick. His voice raw and ragged like he'd swallowed a drill bit.

Just hearing him like that, my heart gave a little jump, as if I'd fi-nally—*finally*—seen the shadow that had been lurking over my shoulder these past few months, the hazard I should have seen coming.

He talked for a while, though with some effort, having to stop and start.

I tried to interject at one point, still in my driveway, my coffee going cold in the center cup holder. Hadn't he sounded fine on Friday? Now here he was, waiting for the results from his COVID test. It was hard for me to imagine he could drag himself into a clinic. Doctors weren't his thing. So how sick was he?

Could *I* be sick?

"Clark, you're not listening." Hayes paused, sounding out of breath. I could hear him cough in the background, his phone clearly turned away. "Gary knew those stucco guys had tested positive. He knew. I was practi-cally beside them Wednesday, Thursday. He didn't say a damn thing to me."

Another cough.

I didn't understand. "Why would he let them work if they were sick?"

Silence on the other end.

"Hayes?"

"That's a dumb question, Clark. You know why."

And I did. But I didn't want to believe it.

The job had to get done.

It always came down to that. The job always had to get done, one way or the other. *Don't like it?* they'd ask. *Should've gotten an office job, then, bud.*

———

I knew where Gary lived; I'd had to pick up blueprints there only the week before. I figured it was about time I paid him a visit. Maybe cough in his face a little.

That's what I was thinking, anyway.

But I didn't go to his place. Still, I couldn't just go back inside my house either, not if I could have the virus too. Maybe I could hole up in the basement, but I wasn't sure.

I needed to think a minute.

I guess that's the difference between me at twenty-two and me now at thirty-eight—I've learned the value of reflection. You can thank Deb for that. She's stitched patience into my heart like a doctor suturing a wound, slowly, one stitch after another, year by year.

So I put my truck in reverse and backed out of the driveway. As I bumped onto the street, my hard hat rolled from the passenger seat into the footwell on the floor, bouncing like an empty turtle shell.

Leaving my subdivision and heading into the city proper, I tried to clear my mind. To just breathe, focus on driving. Since the lockdowns, traffic had been light, even during rush hour, and I was still an hour ahead of even that. The streets were nearly deserted, the intersections interrupted only by my passing.

Anywhere you needed to go, you could get there in record time.

Silver linings, Deb said. I always saw them. Even when I shouldn't.

"Gotta stay positive," I'd tell her.

She'd scowl. "By keeping your head in the sand?"

"By seeing whatever I need to see to get me through the day. See it, be it."

She'd roll her eyes.

Since she'd been off, she'd been learning as much as she could about the virus, precautions we should take, things we should do, when this whole thing might end. She started reading about past pandemics too, scouring the internet while trying to avoid conspiracy schlock. For a week, all I heard about was the Spanish flu, about how the world had made it through World War I only to be hit by a deadly virus.

From studying that pandemic, she knew that we'd probably be in for a second wave with COVID-19, that the second wave would be worse for the number of infected and worse for the number of dead. And when she was proven right, not once did she say, "I told you so."

But there was one factoid that she did bring up more than once. During the Spanish flu, construction workers experienced one of the highest mortality rates. The trauma of war, mixed with hazardous working conditions, left them prime targets. That and the old chestnut that "the job just has to get done, no matter what."

That had hit a little too close to home. Even with this morning's news, you couldn't help but feel that our site's shutdown was too little, too late. We should have shut down weeks ago.

But that bastard Gary.

It was a twenty-minute drive to Dolton Glass and another thirty minutes from there to the job site my crew and I had been working for the past three months. I took a shortcut to the site—as good a place to think as any.

The city streets soon gave way to an old industrial park, factories lining either side of the road, some closed due to the lockdown, some deemed essential and left open. Skeleton crews even then.

A minute later, I was out of the city altogether.

Back roads quickly led to the new builds. Not houses, but commercial buildings—warehouses, factories. All under construction and all one contractor. They'd bitten off more than they could chew even before the pandemic hit. But that was construction. That was always construction.

There were no paved roads here—gravel and dirt, leading to the iron, steel, and concrete carapaces of industry.

They all sat empty now. Heavy grading equipment chained to flatbed trailers. Shipping containers storing tools and supplies now padlocked, their doors set to stay closed for at least a month.

I pulled up alongside our own job site, put the truck in park but let the engine idle, not wanting to stay long. I rolled down the window, and the cold morning air was like needles in my lungs. The building was unfinished, ugly, desolate.

I shook my head and swore.

The loss of work would hurt, but the alternative?

How many of us might be sick? I didn't feel sick yet, but . . .

I thought of Hayes, laid up at home, sounding terrible. Would it get worse for him? It might, it really might. He certainly wasn't at peak physical health.

I frowned, feeling guilt, like a heavy stone strapped to my chest.

Maybe I should have put my foot down weeks ago. But maybe we would have lost the job. Probably would have. There were a handful of other glass companies in the region who'd have been happy to finish for us.

I reached for my coffee, downed nearly half of it in three swallows, then rolled up the truck window. The heater made quick work of the cold inside the cab. I pulled my cell from my pocket and found Gary's number from my contacts.

The phone rang, and rang, and rang.

Not only was Gary not answering, but he'd also disabled his voicemail.

I sighed. Disappointed but not surprised. I downed the rest of my coffee.

Typical Gary. Typical construction.

A month or so into the pandemic, there was a push for the local government to close job sites. And they did, eventually. Well, nonessential ones, anyway. Was anyone surprised when most contractors found a way to declare their sites essential? Hardly. Then when restrictions became more stringent, when the list of what could be classified as essential became more specific, were we at Dolton Glass surprised that good ol' Gary found a way to force us onto site? Nope. He was supposed to close things down well over a month ago, but as long as the work being done was in an effort to "close in" the site so that the inside of the building could not be accessed, then work could continue.

To my mind, closing in a site means throwing some plywood in the openings and calling it a day. To Gary, it meant the trades working on the building's exterior had to fully complete their job, including all our finish work from caulking to drip-sills to sweeps on the doors.

And now here we were with our very own site outbreak.

Hayes was right. Nobody gave a damn about construction workers.

And what was the point of all this? Why did we bust our backs on the regular? We built the houses, the workplaces, ran the electrical and the plumbing, set the windows through which everyone looked out upon the world. Any time someone took a leisurely stroll in their neighborhood, did they ever think of the worker on their knees, smoothing out the sidewalk's concrete by hand for every step that walker took, or every thousand? And now, amid COVID-19, what were we doing here?

I closed my eyes, my jaw tensed, my hands restless against the steering wheel.

When the history books write of this pandemic, there will be a lot of praise for the frontline workers, the doctors and nurses and other hospital staff. And rightly so, but—

On the passenger seat beside me, my phone began to ring.

Well, look who decided to call me back, I thought, feeling smug, feeling anger begin to smoke and smolder in my chest. And I let it, working myself up.

But instead of Gary, it was head office again.

Hayes had tested positive.

My whole crew—all six of us—would need to get COVID tests.

My anger froze, became a cold fear settling in my stomach.

The truck rumbled on, indifferent.

———

It was a small relief when my test came back negative.

On the same day I got the result I also got the news that Hayes had been taken to the hospital. Two of our other guys had also tested positive, but they were faring better.

Deb agreed that I should quarantine in the basement. And when the results came in, she ran down the basement stairs and kissed me so hard I thought my teeth might fall out. There were tears in her eyes when we parted, and I wiped them away with my thumb and then kissed her again.

But it felt perfunctory, insincere. She could tell that something was wrong and didn't need to ask what.

"So what happens now?" she said.

I shrugged. "Nothing."

Dolton Glass was on an indefinite shutdown. Oh, a few of the office staff would work from home, but everyone else was grounded, told to register for unemployment.

It was some surprise then when, three days later, I got a call on my cell, not from the office at all, but from a woman I'd never met. Her voice sounded young and strained. There was noise in the background too. Crying?

"I have a broken window," she said, though it came out sounding like a question.

"Excuse me?"

"Isn't this Dolton Glass? You guys do emergency service, right?" Again there was more noise in the background. I heard a man's voice now as well as a little girl's. The little girl, I think, was who I'd heard crying.

In short order I learned that the woman had called Dolton Glass and been automatically redirected to my cell number. We advertised 24/7 emergency service, and we rotated who was on call, with any incoming calls being directed to the respective employee's number. In all honesty, I'd completely forgotten that it was my week.

I switched my cell to the other ear. "Is this for a business?"

"No, a house. *My* house." She sounded near-panicked. "Can you come? There's glass everywhere. The last two places I called flat out told me no."

"Okay," I said, already trying to figure out what I would tell Deb. "Okay. Let me get your address."

After stopping by the shop to get a work van, it took me another fifteen minutes to get to their home over on the east end of town. It was a two-story semi with an old Hyundai Accent parked in the driveway and a booster seat in the back. The house was red brick from top to bottom with a big bay window on the first floor that stared out at me like the broken mouth of a drunken fighter. Shards of glass lay scattered across the wooden front porch.

Jutting awkwardly out through the hole in the window was one of those cat jungle gyms—a carpeted pole with several shoebox-sized platforms attached at varying heights, good for climbing and scratching. It looked a little worse for wear.

I disinfected my hands, slipped on a face mask, then grabbed my toolbox. The father met me at the door, but kept his distance—he was wearing a mask, too. Deb would be happy to hear that. A brown-and-white cat stood by the man's feet, licking its paws and cleaning its face, as nonplussed as any cat I'd ever seen.

Inside, the living room was in disarray. TV still on, tuned to some children's station. Couch cushions on the floor. A muddy-looking puddle on the coffee table, upturned coffee mug next to it. Then there was the glass, broken shards of it scattered every which way.

A chaos caused by sudden panic.

I was about to discuss the emergency service fee with the dad when I noticed the blood. Several spatters on the jagged edges of the broken window, then several more on the carpet below.

"Someone cut themselves?"

The father nodded. He looked stricken. "My daughter. She cut her hand. Trying to see if the cat was okay." He kept staring at the hole in the window.

"She all right?"

"Yeah, I think so. But, you know . . ." He shrugged, looking at me then looking away. "We didn't want to take her to the hospital. COVID, you know? But . . . well, there was a lot of blood."

I bet there had been. Hands are bleeders, no question.

I set about fixing the window. The glass—a double-paned thermal unit—would have to be ordered; for now all I could do was board up the opening. Still, it was work enough just taking out the broken panes, then cleaning up the shattered glass. I even brought in the shop vacuum from the van, making sure I got every little piece in the living room as well as out on the front porch.

The whole time, the dad watched me from the kitchen, having pulled out a chair from the kitchen table, and turning it around to face me.

"Is there anything I can do?" he said at one point, sounding like he was afraid I might say yes, but also like he felt bad leaving me to do all the work.

I told him no. Truth was, it felt good to be out of the house, working with my hands, doing a job that actually *did* have to get done for once.

By the time I had the plywood cut and fitted into the opening, both the mom and daughter had joined their father in the kitchen, the whole crew of them watching silently, the daughter hiding behind her mom's leg, all of them in face masks.

"That should do it," I said once the last of the window trim had been nailed back in place. I returned my tools to my toolbox, dusted my hands on the knees of my work pants.

The daughter whispered something to her mom.

"You can tell him," the mom said, giving her daughter a gentle nudge. "Go on."

The little girl, likely no older than five or six, came from around her mom's leg, but not out of her reach. Her red hair was in tiny pigtails, and she was already in her pajamas. Her eyes were downcast, but after a moment she lifted her gaze to meet mine. I could see she'd been crying. "thankyou."

It was barely louder than a whisper, worse with her mask.

But I heard it louder than church bells. It feels silly to say it, but I almost felt like crying right then and there myself. Big baby, I guess. Or just grateful for the gratitude, maybe. This pandemic had left me—and plenty of other trades workers—feeling used up and discarded.

I saw that the girl was favoring her left hand, which was neatly wrapped in white bandage.

I motioned to it. "I heard you cut yourself."

She nodded.

"And I bet it hurts. I've cut myself a few times too over the years." I held my hands out to show her, turning them over from front to back.

She had to strain to see from where she stood, but her eyes widened at the lines of scar writ across my skin, most of which I'd earned when I was still new to the trade.

"It can hurt in the beginning. But not for long," I told her. "Cuts heal. And these scars? They tell stories of your adventures, of who you are. And I bet you've already had some adventures of your own. Am I right?"

I got a meager nod, but I could see the slight smile in her eyes.

"You and your daddy?" I asked.

"And my mommy," she answered back, almost defiantly.

Both her parents laughed.

"What do you say to the nice man?" her mom said again.

The little girl thought it over, her eyebrows knitting together, as if it was serious business.

Finally, what she settled on, and very matter-of-factly, was: "Maybe you should wear gloves."

We all laughed at that, me probably the hardest.

And when I hopped back in the work van and pulled off my mask, I felt better than I had in a long time. I tried to settle myself in that feeling.

It was as if I knew it wouldn't last.

———

This is how I imagined what happened next, the fantasy that I scribbled out in my head and then committed to memory. It makes sense. It feels complete.

Maybe it's true.

Over the next few weeks there were a handful of other emergency calls, but not many. With everybody staying inside, fewer windows were getting broken. Still, Dolton Glass divvied up the work, paying the guys in cash. I had two more calls of my own.

Other than that, I stayed home except for groceries and gas.

I stopped at the drug store once, too.

Maybe that's where I caught it.

I can't be sure.

All I know is I woke up on a Wednesday morning feeling like I could cook an egg on top of my head, that's how hot it felt. I tried to jump out of bed, keep myself away from Deb. What I managed was more of a pathetic sprawl over the side and onto the bedroom floor.

Still, I sequestered myself in the basement, told her to stay on the top levels.

"Be safe." I told her.

"I love you," she called back.

I had a fever, though not as bad as I'd feared.

Five days passed like that. The cough never came, the fever abated. But I didn't trust myself to come up, not yet. Be safe, I told myself.

On the sixth day, as I was staring blankly at the TV, watching but not watching a rerun of *Dr. Phil*, I heard a wrap on the basement window. I nearly filled my pants, I kid you not.

It was Thomas Hayes hunched over, staring back at me through the glass, looking like some Hells Angel come to rob me. I couldn't help but grin.

He held up his phone. I understood immediately and answered the moment I saw him punch in the call. It's how we would speak to each other.

"Hospital let you out?" I said.

His voice was gruff and a bit raw sounding, but better. He nodded through the window. "Only for you to take my place, it seems. Deb tells me you've locked yourself up."

"Better safe than sorry," I said.

He laughed at that. "From you to God's ears. You tell Gary as much? He might learn a thing or two."

"First thing out of my mouth next time I see him. Doubt he'll listen, though."

"Nobody cares about us construction workers, right?" He shrugged. "Except for us. You and me. The guys."

It almost sounded like he was going soft on me. "Maybe that's enough, huh?"

He chuffed. "Nope. But it's a damn start."

I suppose it was. Better than nothing.

"See you in a bit, then," Hayes said.

And I nodded. "Soon as I can."

He put his fist to the smooth glass of the basement window, his knuckles old and gnarled. It took me half a second to understand that he wanted to bump. It was all we could do.

I touched my fist to the glass, thinking I'd won ol' Hayes over after all.

But the glass was cold.

―――――

Because what actually happened was as anticlimactic as it was inevitable.

It's not how I had imagined it would go.

I never got sick. What I got was a phone call.

And not from someone needing help. No little girl needing a pick-me-up.

It was a phone call from the head office again, but this time from the boss himself. And not first thing in the morning, but halfway through the afternoon while I was washing dishes at the kitchen sink, thinking of nothing while my eyes followed our dog as he roamed the backyard.

Thomas Hayes had died the night before.

Because of the lockdown, there would be no funeral. No memorial service either. He'd died alone at the hospital. His wife was devastated. There'd be a collection taken up to help her out.

I ended the call and stood there, not knowing what to do.

I could hear Deb upstairs, folding laundry, humming to herself. Safe.

But I stared down at my hands, flexed the fingers, looked for the stories there written in lines of scar tissue.

For the life of me, I couldn't read anything there at all.

Poetry | *Robert Okaji*

POSTCARD FROM PANDEMIC

———

They stack their cart with essentials:
frozen garlic, six packages of grilled
mushrooms, fifteen cans of garbanzo
beans, three bottles of truffle oil and
enough alkaline water to float a fleet
of dinghies. There is, alas, no hand
sanitizer, no toilet paper. You must
decide, he says, between the jar of
organic marinara and the 2% milk.
Weighing need against desire she
chooses the sauce, then selects a
bundle of the brightest daffodils.

———

Previously published in *Vox Populi*

Poetry | *Vanessa Chica Ferreira*

A CLASSROOM HUMS IN WAIT.

———

In the Bronx
In an old but sturdy building
There is an empty classroom
There are many empty classrooms
But that one is mine

An invitation of blues/yellows
Sky/Sun
Marjoram/peppermint clouds
A crisp bite of citrus

If you ever been you would agree

An overflowing sea of creation
The drawings of tiny hands, each a world of its own
Mathematical equations
Numbers that make sense after weeks and weeks of practice

A perfect square of life and dust
A vibrant messy blessing

A makeshift teacher desk holds
A surplus of data
A never ending "to-do" list
A cup that states "Teaching is a work of heart"
A heart-shaped pen

Gifts from little ones that echo
Love

There is an empty classroom
It is not quiet
It is not abandoned
It hums in wait
laughter skips across its walls
I hear it from miles away
An energy that lingers . . .

SICKNESS: *My stomach charley-horsed*

"HOLD YOUR BREATH," WATERCOLOR, MIXED MEDIA

MICHAL MITAK MAHGEREFTEH, 2020

MY COVID STORY

———

January 2020

After serving just over twenty-eight years of a life sentence, I had finally made parole. I was overjoyed! All I had to do was complete an eighteen-month rehabilitation program and I would be free.

I first heard about the virus on the evening news. How it was killing people in Wuhan, China, a world away. Never in my wildest dreams did I think this novel Coronavirus called COVID-19 would come all the way around the world and infect me.

Late February 2020

Word spread around the prison that we were on lockdown. Rumor was that one of the guards had come down with COVID-19. The guard, whose name was never revealed, had supposedly never come into the prison since getting sick. This lockdown was just a precautionary measure. We ate johnnies (sack lunches of one peanut butter and jelly and one meat sandwich) for fourteen days and had to stay in our cells. After fourteen days and nobody reported being sick, we were let up and normal operations were resumed, or the new normal, which meant social distancing and being told to wash hands and eventually being given homemade masks that prisoners in the garment factories made.

Early March 2020

The whole prison was tested for COVID-19 with the mouth swab test. Mine came back negative. While we were waiting on the test results one of the guards who had been working the day of the testing came down sick with COVID-19. Some positive test results came back among the prisoner population as well, but I don't know how many. We went back on lockdown. The nurses started coming by every morning, taking everyone's temperature and heart rate. April and May passed. I was supposed to start my rehabilitation program in May, but the prison system wouldn't transfer me to my program unit because of COVID-19 and fear of its spread.

June comes and goes, and we are told people are still coming down sick but who knows, half of what you hear on Inmate.com turns out to be false. I'm wondering how this is going to affect my going home.

July 2020

They decide to test us all again. The day of the test, I start coughing, just a small dry cough at this point. By the next day, I'm starting to feel different, kind of dizzy or lightheaded. By the third day I noticed that my sense of smell and taste, although not completely gone, was definitely off. Day 4 I was standing in line waiting to go to the shower and felt that I might fall over. I didn't. I made it to the shower and back and made the decision that I was going to report my illness to the authorities. When I did, I was taken to the COVID (evaluation room) where my vitals were taken. The nurse told me they were going to put me in lock-up for evaluation. I was thrown into a solitary cell with no mattress or bedding. I sat on the hard cold steel unable to sleep for over twenty-four hours before they finally brought me a mattress. I had begged every guard that passed my cell to get me a mattress. When it came time to eat, they cracked my door just enough to throw my paper sack on the floor and then would take off, afraid of catching COVID.

On the third day, they told me to pack my stuff, I was moving. I was terribly sick, by this point I was physically wiped out, totally exhausted. I hadn't eaten a bite in two days and was having terrible coughing fits so bad that at one point my stomach charley-horsed.

I was made to drag my five bags of personal property to the opposite end of the prison to 12 dorm, a dorm that had been turned into a COVID patient residence. After a few days there, we were moved again to 11 dorm, another COVID dorm. By this time I was having severe body aches on top of everything else, especially my back and calves. Also my feet and the tip of my left index finger would get hot.

Every day I told the nurses I hadn't eaten in days and that I was having coughing fits, but it went in one ear and out the other. They told me to get some nonaspirin from the guard.

About day 10, I started having difficulty breathing. I could only take shallow breaths and my urine was dark as coffee. I put my little desk fan right in front of my face blowing air up my nostrils, which helped me a lot. And I got some Chlorophan which helped me, especially with the coughing.

Around day 15 I started feeling better and by day 20 I was back to my old self for the most part with the exception of lingering fatigue and the occasional cough.

I survived where some didn't. We had three people die at that prison. Fortunately, I wasn't one of them.

On August 4, 2020, I was transferred here to my rehabilitation, where in eighteen months I will walk out the door a free man. I'm excited about my second chance at life and look forward to the future.

———

The events in this essay occurred at the Ramsey unit of the Texas Department of Criminal Justice, Rosharon, Texas.

Poetry | *Lavinia Kumar*

ESSENTIALLY UNSEEN

I disinfect, remove trash and refresh supplies
says Maria, hospital cleaner twenty years
I find my job rewarding because I empathize.

Rita, now 67, had retired, says
to look after patients is why I'm back here
as she cleans, disinfects, provides fresh supplies.

Environmental Services daily on the front line,
dress simply, not in "professional" gear,
find their jobs rewarding because they empathize.

Patient Jason thanked Rosaura—he so agonized
she talked with him, gave him strength to fight,
came near to him when she brought fresh supplies.

And some days Essential Workers take extra time
to discuss how plots are turning on the TV
because there are no visitors. And they empathize.

Ezzie, a cancer survivor, now is terrified
I'm the only one working. My husband was fired.
She disinfects, removes trash, refreshes supplies,
says, *there are many unseen workers on the front lines.*

NUDGE

————

These days,
The mornings
Look like the aftermath
Of a midnight rush.
I stumble out of bed,
My eyes are weary
With twenty minutes to spare.

Lately, I haven't been able to sleep.
Words are eating my insides
Forming an allegiance,
Creating unconscious gold
That unravel in
My collection of notes.

"ECLIPSE," DIGITAL COLLAGE AND ILLUSTRATION
ILARIA CORTESI, 2020 | PREVIOUSLY PUBLISHED IN *BARZAKH*

ELEGY

———

"The hearing is the last
to go," they tell us
but we have stopped listening
to anything other than his body
breathing. Next to me, I hear
my mother promising to love beyond
this world and my face is wet and hot
and hurting. I hear my father's laugh
in the echoes of some memory:
mi reina, mi güera. His ghost
in my ears. We have begun to play
his favorite songs, the ones he always sang
the wrong words to but no one cares
about that now. The last thing we hope he hears
is the ocean & the sound of his boat's hull
hitting a small wave and the seagulls—
god, I hope he hears the seagulls.

———

Previously published in *New York Quarterly*

Poetry | *Joan E. Bauer*

I CUT UP MY HILLARY T-SHIRT
TO MAKE A COVID MASK

———

—for Anthony Fauci, MD

The most trusted man is grandfatherly, slight
of build, bespectacled. Brooklyn accent.

He warns us not to touch our face.
He rubs his forehead. We anxiously await:

Just tell us what to do. No sugarcoating.

The grandson of immigrants grew up
in Italian-Jewish Bensonhurst,

rode his bike delivering the meds prescribed
by his pharmacist father. The family lived

above the drugstore. Just 80 minutes each way
by bus & subway stop to the Catholic high school

in Manhattan that prepared him for Holy Cross.
The Jesuits taught him Latin, Greek, & philosophy.

Just a few years ahead of Billy Collins.
First in his class at Cornell Med, but something

more than science gave him the gift to truly see
the humanity of his patients.

During the AIDS epidemic, he'd take any punch
Larry Kramer gave him. *Angry, damn right!*

He walked into Castro District bath houses,
earned the trust of those at risk, those afflicted,

urged them into clinical trials that saved
who-knows-how-many lives. Now he stands

before a reckless president, explaining
patiently, painstakingly—the prognosis.

Previously published in *Infection House*

**"LISTENING TO A STREET PREACHER AND WAITING FOOD
AT CHURCH RELIEF CENTER," PHOTOGRAPH**
TOM DARIN LISKEY, 2020

Fiction | *Waliyah Oladipo*

A STORY OF CONSTANTINE, COVID-19, AND PANDORA

———

A question Constantine asks gets me strangely excited. It is a gutsy question, one that no one else has asked me before. It makes my heart race. I try to see if I can make out the beats to the violent dance in my chest.

His gaze is so direct, the exact opposite of my oscillatory pupil movement. Constantine asks again, and I can see his frustration rising. He asks, "Are you happy?"

———

The screech of the car pulls me forward in my seat before I settle with a bounce. I pull my eyes off of my phone screen and look up to see what the commotion is about. Turns out it's no commotion at all, it's just another sign of inactivity, a blocked road ahead.

A security officer, who looks sixty and some, stands by in a green uniform, his hands in his pocket as he peers down at my mother in the driver's seat.

She offers her sheepish smile and rolls down the window a bit.

"Ẹ̀kú iṣẹ́ sir, I didn't know the road was blocked," she says.

The man does not move, either he is not Yoruba, or he refuses to be charmed by a pretty face and a nice car. I am amused.

As a last resort, my mother begins to reverse, she makes sure to go slowly, punctuating the movement with loud friendly words about how it's going to take her forever to turn.

To my dismay, the man gives up very easily. He raises a hand to stop my mother from pretending to have the car in reverse.

147

She grins eagerly and turns to me.

"Nice man. Do you think I should tip him?"

"No, I don't," I say emphatically.

My mother gives me a second to change my mind—as if I have any real say in the matter—but I don't. That man was easy, too easy. Besides, I am sick and tired of the tradition of tipping everyone, which directly corresponds to bribing them around here.

Ahead of the car, the man raises the large chunk of metal, then lifts his hand again, opening and fisting it thrice, and my mom quickly zooms by.

———

It's day 5 and I am yet to give Constantine an answer, partly because I don't want to lose the tap in my chest every time he asks, and partly because it's the one thing that keeps Constantine interested; my tailored smiles, my non-answers, my compounding silence.

———

My thoughts are disrupted by how near we are to our destination. Left to me, I don't want to go, but these things have never been left to me.

———

I was seventeen when I was first diagnosed with hepatitis C. Sometimes I resent my mother and her obsession with going to the hospital for so many tests. If she had not taken me, I never would have known. I bet there are so many people on the street who walk around with worse health conditions and live their lives in ignorant bliss and die a silent death. No one suspects a thing.

But it's hard to keep up the resentment, it's hard when I remember the months of 7:00 a.m. to 4:00 p.m. appointments at University College Hospital, in light of trying to get a diagnosis, when we sat side by side at the waiting room of SOP, arranging and rearranging our clothes so that nothing touched the floor or another sick person. There were days we went hungry because, in a bid to meet our appointment, we left the house too early to even prepare tea. We were always afraid of catching something from the illegal hawkers squeaking past the waiting rooms and offices. At times, we shared laughter with others, because it's not always gloom on those floors. Other times, we got angry at rude nurses who seemed to take a special delight in misplacing hospital files and sneaking someone's name before mine. But my mother was there, she was my support.

My father was there too, he was the money bank. Getting a diagnosis was as much a curse as it was a blessing. On the good side, I knew where I stood. My liver was still good enough, my sugar level was great, my kidney was fine. On the other side, we pumped so much money into tests: liver function tests today, virality tests tomorrow. There was a constant availability of examinations to pay for. Sometimes, I would turn around and catch my father staring at me, and in those moments, I wondered what he was thinking, if he resented me a little bit.

The doctors kept changing, but each was as friendly as the last. They were always too eager to pull me into a law versus medicine argument. I often let them. It was easier than listening in on the other doctors in the room, telling someone they needed a transplant, or a five-hundred-thousand-naira operation.

It was easy to forget whenever I was in uni, staying in my hostel, excited by classes and the steady supply of novel mischief. But Fridays were horror days. I always had to carry the yellow cooler with orange tingeing the top. I hid the shame in my bag as I went to class, I was always half listening, waiting for 11:45 when I would have to disappear. At noon came the religious hour of viral worship.

Even before that time, I would grow impatient, and my friends would send me knowing glances. My friends knew, there is no way to hide something like that from your closest friends. At 11:45, I would carry my cooler out of class, hail a cab from uni and head straight to the hospital. I was always late but the nurses had learned to tolerate me, some even liked me. It was quite easy, getting an ice-cold liquid injected straight into my thigh and returning to school with my cooler.

The only downside was the disfigurement of my thigh, but it wasn't so hard to cut myself off from wearing short skirts and gowns. It earned me the "good girl" tag.

I lived my life like that for one year, constantly taking tests, constantly getting disappointed, secretly throwing out expensive pills, constantly tired and in pain. But there was hope, and that hope got me through, until one day when I decided I didn't need hope anymore.

The years breezed by, I blissfully ignored everything, every voice in my head that tried to tell me these things don't just go away. The pain that came on very rare days was easy to overlook in the face of studying and constant laughter, of steady doses of gossip and my love life.

———

I am lured out of my thoughts by the sound of the engine dying. The first thing I notice is that the building is different from the one I am used to. I roll down the window and stretch out my head to look around for a name. It reads Pandora and I laugh out loud from the gut at the absurdity. I instantly decide I like this diagnostics center.

"Why are you laughing?" my mom asks, surprised at my sudden change of mood.

"The name of the place."

She looks at me strangely and I mutter a never mind as I glide out of the car.

"Don't touch anything," she snaps, as my hands begin to descend on the hood of the car.

"Not even our car?" I say, falling into step beside her.

"Not even 'my' car."

"But you disinfect it every morning, you use Dettol."

My mother just nods her head in greeting to the security officer and ignores me. Knowing her, she probably believes that a pedestrian's sneeze may have landed on her car while we drove here, and this pedestrian may have coronavirus.

I am not surprised when we are met outside with a hastily built handwashing station, designed with rushed graffiti about coronavirus and precautions. I go first. I hit the button for the soap and proceed to wash. I open the tap with my elbow for water, but my mother comes through, "That's barely sixteen seconds."

How is this woman not a spokesperson for the virus yet? Amused, I complete my four seconds and rinse, then wait for her to have the cycle.

As soon as we get to the reception, our hands are bathed with sanitizers again, and my mom nods as she rubs her hands together, pleased that extreme measures are being taken. We are made to answer questions about travel histories and symptoms. At this point, I am just bored. I reply no five times and the masked and gloved receptionist finally seems to relax. I wonder if this is how she tenses up all day, if she crunches up her shoulders every time someone walks through the door. Her job mustn't be easy, being forced to stare an aggressive virus in the face.

I take a survey of the room, a man flings his arms across a cushion. He has a suspended injection crafted around his left palm. Another man is turned on his side, making a call, his other hand firmly holds his sneaky little daughter in place. There are others, all different, but united by failing health.

I wonder if we catch coronavirus by leaving our homes and coming to this red zone, if we are more likely to die from the virus rather than our actual sickness. I wonder if any of us can do anything about it.

My mom arranges herself again and words gush out of me before I can stop them. "If being here bothers you so much, you should have listened to me and waited until the coronavirus ends."

She sends me her icy glare. "And that will be when? Don't get me angry, Tinuade."

I am surprised she isn't already. After all, I have been pushing it all morning. If only she hadn't looked into my eyes and seen their irritating, pervading yellow that could have been avoided if my weight hadn't dropped by six kilograms in a few weeks. Everyone who saw me had a comment or two about how thin I have become.

"Ọrùn ẹ ti dí kòtò, oò jẹun ni?"

If not for all of that, I could have gone on hiding all the signs that have been there for three weeks. The extreme fatigue, the yellow palms, the unfiltered urine color, the slight temperature, nausea. I was dealing with it all by drinking water and desperately praying. That should have been enough.

So this morning, when she announced that I dress up and we head to the hospital, it was a war. I raved and protested, I reminded her that the hospital was the most dangerous place right now. She called my doctor (whose number I shouldn't have been surprised she still has) who then ordered me to go for the test. When my father added in his overbearing weight, I had no choice but to surrender.

A rising noise at the wash station outside pulls me back into the reception area. The wash station officer is screaming at a man to wash his hands. The man insists that the wash station procedure is more dangerous to him, as so many people have used it, so he will stick to his sanitizer. The wash station officer pushes down his nose mask and begins to explain that the man can use his sanitizer after observing the compulsory procedure. Said man begins to shout at everybody, "Do you all know who I am? I am calling the hospital director immediately."

Wash station officer completely rids himself of his mask and begins to beat his chest in rapid succession. A nurse suddenly begins to cry, and another nurse holds her.

Just as things are getting more interesting, the receptionist calls my name. I tap my mother who appears to be so thoroughly engrossed in the unsolicited drama that she doesn't hear the receptionist.

"What test?"

"LFT."

"Just that?"

I glare at her, and she quickly spells out the price. I am slightly worried that it's a lot more than it used to be, but my mother seems to have fully anticipated the turn of things and counts the required cash out of her bag.

A man appears out of nowhere in a lab coat and a face mask, and he looks so hot that I instantly wish I didn't come here with my mother. He even has a sexy voice.

He asks my mother if she would rather wait for me in the reception and for a minute, a promise rises. But my mother shakes her head firmly and informs him that she has "to ensure everything you use for the test is new."

I roll my eyes in disappointment. Not only has she stopped me from having a chance to get hotcake's number, but she also ensures she renders me twelve while at it.

Hotcake directs us to a squeaky clean examination room, and to my disappointment, it's another person who is to take my test. My mother watches like a hawk.

She tries, in the way of an overeager microbiologist, to strike up a conversation. She fails.

As the nurse finally finds a willing vein to draw my blood from, she opens her mouth again.

"Come on, don't look so grim. It's just LFT."

"Have you ever paid weekly for an injection that costs one month of the feeding allowance of your entire familywhich, mind you, comprises six people?"

After that, we had a relatively quiet time.

"Your result will be ready tomorrow."

That makes my mother unhappy. "Why? In our former testing center, it used to take just a day."

"COVID-19 . . . ," the overeager microbiologist mutters.

I wonder just how much more COVID-19 will have to take responsibility for.

I mutter my thanks and head out. To my disappointment, the commotion outside has died out. The wash station officer is back in his mask, the angry personal sanitizer man is nowhere in sight. The two nurses by default have disappeared too.

My mother anoints me with her sanitizer before unlocking the car. I slide into the car, grateful for the different air. I unlock my phone and begin to reading.

"I am happy, I am happy because I am. Because despite the madness that constantly invades my home, I have moments when I am nothi? but a seventeen year old. Because even though my future is uncl? can enjoy the company of a friend, I can laugh and mean it. I ar/

because I refuse to be bitter, I am happy because I choose what happiness means."

"Is that enough?" Constantine asks. "Don't you want more?"

Of course, I do. Why wouldn't I?

"At times, it is. To be happy is not to wallow in contentment. Happiness isn't a state of permanence, it's assurance in finding a reason to go on tomorrow, a willingness to be surprised, enjoying what is. It's just the opposite of pain, and pain, if still felt by the conscious, cannot be permanent either."

The next week when the test results came, the doctor recommended Coartem for chronic malaria.

NEW AGE

———

Fingering the tourmaline amulet
strung around her neck, she hopes to channel
a "plasma"—ethereal and healing—
that might resuscitate her blood. Doctors,

who've perused her corpuscles many times
these months, still offer the same prognosis:
strange invaders in her veins. Neither
holistic medicine, cognitive

therapy, nor harmonic convergence
have managed to eradicate the plague
that's ground her life to dust. *She is my friend,*
I think, *and she is crazy.* I am caught

between a rock and a sacred place,
trying, pathetically, to comfort her
within the bounds of what I consider
rational and sane. She tells me Librans

are known for their recuperative powers.
I nod. After lunch, she hugs me goodbye,
then grabs me, hard. This is not about sex.
It is, though, about bodies—healthy ones

that have not rebelled. She looks up at me
for a sign. *What a lunatic*, I think,
even while I hold her as hard as I can,
trying to be a crystal for her fear.

Previously published in *The Paris Review*

Poetry | *Deidra Suwanee Dees*

ALCOHOL WOMAN

———

painful childhood of neglect,
abandonment, stealing
the last remnant of my Indianness

alcohol woman breezed back to
the rez
twenty-two winters later

without warning, dropping by my trailer
gifting me with expensive
leather photo album, my encircled
baby picture
glowers on the cover,

alone,
body draped with liquor-laden time,
newly swallowed by COVID-19
miserable attempt to play
the mother role she sold for libation,
nothing from me,
awkwardly shuffling out the door,

agony runs through my
consciousness, untamed horses
stamping out my existence,

collecting my senses, reminding
myself time had gnawed off the edge,

figured out how to live without
a mother or a father,
desperately needed a mother back then,

irrelevant
COVID reckoning, misery was paid
—alcohol woman is *not needed now,*

accomplishments . . .
amassing strength from childhood
toys of adversity and peril

remembering how far I've come

on my own . . . garbage can gulps down

a cheap

leather photo album

Previously published in *SFWP Quarterly*

GRIEF: *Interjected like a comma*

"FAMILY HIT BY JOB LOSS RECEIVING FOOD, FLOWERS FROM CHURCH," PHOTOGRAPH • TOM DARIN LISKEY, 2020

Poetry | *Emily Ransdell*

ELEGY, INTERRUPTED

———

—for Kay

I have tried hard to do what's right,
following the arrows down the grocery's
one-way aisles, staying six feet away
from anything that breathes.
I've made masks from old bandanas,
wear mascara to look bright-eyed on Zoom.
How are you doing, asks everyone.
Sometimes I forget you are dead.
To grieve for anyone is to grieve
for everyone—the hundreds of thousands now.
I'm ashamed to admit I haven't cried.
To kill time in lockdown I scroll through photos,
Christmas after Christmas of us
looking older, summer after summer
in more sensible hats.
No service, no wake, this is the way
we grieve now,
solitary and without ceremony,
not even a thrift shop open
to take your clothes.

MY MOTHER WHISPERS, DOESN'T HE LOOK SO PEACEFUL

In wake of my father's funeral
I imagine my own body buried
under gritty guilt earth,
a ticking tomb.

There, my father's dreams suffocated in a casket—
silver, gold-lined, and stiff. He has always been
a light sleeper and I am aching
to wake him.

Poetry | *Bianca Alyssa Pérez*

A SONNET FOR THE LIVING

This empty casket of stagnant grief
feels like melted wax and little flame.
Like the darkest night, an endless deep disease
touching everything with the sharp claws of shame.
My days now have nothing to do with smiles
so, I pick orange bulbing marigolds
from the tender earth and for a while
I forget my heart beating angry, rotting mold.
While Death, like a plate of salt, sits thirsty
and waiting, La Santa Muerte bears a womb
of insatiable appetite and we pray for mercy
and, at the very least, a comfortable tomb.
    For this is a sonnet for the living,
    Tender-hearted and reminiscing.

"EDGE OF THE FOREST," OIL AND GOUACHE ON 100% RAG PAPER
CAROLINE FURR, 2020

#COVIDCLARITY

———

I have been constrained in this Harlem apartment for the last twelve months. Perhaps constrained is a harsh word to use, but it is a harsh time. Nothing seems fair or equitable about this virus. People have claimed that it is the great equalizer; I believe it is the great illuminator. It illuminates all the crevices of our sordid lives—both as individuals— and as a society as a whole.

Since mid-March 2020, my two sons arrived home from college in Rhode Island for spring break and did not leave. It is a tight space; really for one, maybe two people. Normally my husband and I share the space with little issue—there are four rooms plus a tiny bathroom which measures roughly 5 by 3.5 feet. It's a railroad apartment where one room literally runs into another, like compartments on a train. There are no passages—really, very little privacy. Yet there we were living together in this space for almost five months. Don't get me wrong: I am more than grateful that I could have the three people I love most in the world safely under one roof with me; but it was not cute.

I am an only child, as is my husband. My older kid is an extrovert and my younger is an introvert. Since this self-containment started, the boys and I were on Zoom calls all day—they were technically still at school and I am faculty at a university in the city.

Their stepdad is a nurse at a public hospital in Harlem. When the COVID crisis hit, he was transferred to an open ICU facility in the hospital. God above . . . when he left for work, I watched transfixed as the world we knew transformed before our very eyes; watched the structure of society as we knew it crumble before us in the East and in Europe, knowing that people were dying by the droves in hospital corridors, on the streets; realized that there were no beds left in hospitals, no protective gear for hospital staff and that in the United States, it was coming for us.

In my family cocoon, we were hyper everything. Hyper-vigilant, hyper-clean, hyper-sensitive, hyper-careful with ourselves and each other. All the feelings were no doubt percolating within each of us and I know that mostly I did not know how to articulate them aloud. Most days my husband would work ridiculous hours and make it home to sleep a few hours (sometimes he did not make it home), then get up the next morning to do a wash, rinse, repeat of the day before. It felt to me that we were all doing that; days ran into each other. *Wash, rinse, repeat.*

After the first month I could feel myself unravel emotionally. All the smart moves I made; masked and gloved early morning grocery shopping, contactless deliveries, and surreptitiously avoiding anyone in public spaces started to grate on my very last nerve. My husband exhausted himself physically and emotionally as I tried to hold the household together. I am not built for domesticity, which is why I love my job and its flexibility. Staying indoors, cooking, and cleaning started to grate on me. My sons grated on me. My oldest was in his final year of college. He had Zoom classes and was stuck indoors. Both sons played video games till 5 a.m. each day. And though I theoretically understood that the video games were the way they connected with peers and friends, speaking and surviving unreal worlds, I was annoyed. In the middle of the night on the way to the bathroom they were so loud! I would chastise myself . . . what else would a twenty-two- and twenty-year-old do? They were just being as normal as they could in a very abnormal situation. And still, I was so grateful to have them with me, safe at home. So grateful.

My husband's growing paranoia around the disease wore on me. What did I expect from someone who worked in an open ICU? What could I say to someone who watched as people came in with a cough and then did not make it home, who saw his colleagues get infected and become patients in the ICU? How could I hold it all together?

Everything chafed on me and it left me in shreds. I'm one of those people who cry everyday—happy or sad—my emotions run free and yet I felt so off balance, so outside of myself that I knew I needed therapy. I am an avid believer of good therapy but had not seen someone in years.

On one of my surreptitious walks around the neighborhood I saw a wall sign: *"It's never too late."* Counselling services. Thank God. I emailed and made a virtual appointment. Five minutes into the first session and I was satisfied that we connected well. Mid-April—just one month into the mayhem. Cognitive behavioral therapy is pragmatic—there is homework. It suits me well.

In late April I started looking at this disease and the consequences of the forced shut-in as an opportunity for some clarity around my life. My trio started rolling their eyes at me because I would say: "This is a moment of #covidclarity"—and I would say the word "hashtag" aloud. They did not appreciate me for it. I'm not sure I appreciated myself for it, but it felt like I was on some sort of automatic mode. I guess I believed that if I was able to say the words out loud, then others could listen, if not hear them. At least I said them, right? At least it was real, right? Not just going around my head in a maelstrom.

In my first session with my therapist, she asked me to spell out three stressors. I hesitated. Take your time, she said. I sighed heavily and said I would just say them as I feel, ok? I'm afraid for my husband, I lack productivity, and it feels like I'm grieving my mom's death all over again. And I'm not writing. There seems to be no motivation. I feel like I'm stuck in a bad rendition of the movie *Groundhog Day*—that no matter what I try, the same thing happens day after day after day, and all the days run into each other and I can't tell the difference between Monday and Saturday anymore. As I'm babbling, the tears are running down my face—just pouring down in rivers mingling with my snot as it pools first at my upper lip. This woman who I have just met online sits quietly and watches me with serious eyes.

"Write that down," she says. She sits wordlessly as I make bullet points in my journal. She then says there's a name for this: *situational depression.*

"Oh," I say as I start mopping up the messy snot and tears from my face. "Oh . . ."

I start sobbing again. Wildly. I'm babbling stuff about missing and needing my mom. She died roughly two years ago in March 2018. "I'm sorry," I tell my therapist, "I don't know what's come over me." I can taste the mucous in the back of my throat as I gulp my way through my swallowing, gulping down my feelings, but the words come out of my mouth, broken and gasping for air as if seeking a life of their own—like the birth of some misshapen thing. "I'm sorry," I mumble again.

"It's okay," she says. "There is no limit to grief."

There it is: #covidclarity. . . . There is *no* limit to grief. "And it's ok for that to sit with you, to let it wash over you," she says. "It's ok. Write it down," she says. "Attach that grief to something. Give it a home."

TRAPPED

———

';

//'

/my body has not been

cleaned for

many days

—smell of my own body grease

trapped inside

cotton clothing,

decomposing dishes

    overflowing my

sink,

nightmare of

    COVID-nineteen

invades me

LOVE, CORONAVIRUS

If you were here, I'd be disinfecting everything,
even our lips before we kissed.

Instead, I lie in a quiet bed alone,
reach out to unrumpled sheets.

Writing about you is harder than life under quarantine.
To distract myself I think about making coffee,

then remember I don't drink coffee anymore,
not since the weeks of your dying.

Every time I made coffee after that
you were still dead. Now I drink raw cacao—

at least the bitterness has few associations,
although the fact that it's a superfood,

good for the immune system, makes it suspect.
I have to scroll quickly past the stories

about lung failure and ventilators.
They lead too swiftly to the whoosh

of the machine that kept your lungs inflating,
deflating, inflating even after you were dead.

I told the nurse you were still breathing.
She shook her head sadly. "It's the machine."

"Turn it off," I said, and she did.
Then it was just you and me and your body

and the rain on the ICU window pane
and silence roaring like a cyclone.

It's spring outside again, like then.
I've been inside for weeks.

The empty lot outside is filled with wildflowers—
you should be out there with your camera.

I talk out loud to you when the kid's not around,
and sometimes when he is. He asks me,

"Mom, are you all right?"
It's hard to answer.

I keep my phone on at night
in case someone needs to call,

in case someone is dying.
I can't save anyone, but at least I can listen.

Sometimes at 3 a.m. I get up
searching for a way to burn away the grief,

but it's an insoluble problem.
The whole world is grieving now.

All I can do is lie here trying to breathe,
breathing without you.

Previously published by San Fedele Press, *Art in the Time of COVID-19*, 2020

A POET ATTEMPTS TO HOMESCHOOL, WEEK 6: FRACTIONS

———

To make ocean,
add earth.

To make earth,
add air.

To make air,
add tears, ½ cup.

—

Half of half is
nothing.

To get the total,
do not add halves.

To get the total,
subtract all halves.

—

Add back:
light
consequence

gusset
plume

—

Half the ocean is coral.
Half the sky is geese,
containing multitudes.

—

Half of me is ocean.
Half of me is sky.

—After Tom Petty

Previously published in *Soundings East*

EVAPORATING VILLANELLE DURING
A TIME OF PANDEMIC

Grief arrives often into the middle
of things, interjected like a comma
that survives, woven into the saddle

of a list chosen by Oxford for battle,
twanging every axon in the soma.
Grief arrives often into the middle

and rarely softens,
demagoguery
that survives, woven

into the sodden
season, sharp-eyed, spry.
Grief arrives, sudden

serrated knives.
Fabric frayed
that survives—

defended;
amended.
Grief arrives.
That survives.

With inspiration from EMOTION #2 by Walter Brown. Previously published in *Under a Warm Green Linden*, Issue 9, Summer 2020

A DAY IN THE LIFE

———

Currently we are on a precautionary COVID-19 lockdown and have been on restrictive movement for several months now. All taking place during a "Texas Summer," and we are inarguably (for which there is essentially no argument) in the hottest month now, August. Brutal heat, limited phone use, limited movement, limited food, and last but nowhere least, no visits allowed from loved ones. All in the name of paying a debt to society. A debt being paid by almost two million people in US prisons, most of whom have received a harsh sentence. Paying almost exactly double the debt owed. While I fully understand there is no place in society for a criminal, I also fully understand when a punishment goes above and beyond its intended purpose. I've met a multitude of men who deserve to go home only to get denied countless times by a broken and outdated parole system. These are the conditions faced by us daily.

I leave you with a picture. The picture is of a man sitting in a tin shed and the sun is beating down on him relentlessly. And while the sun is causing him to suffer, he also longs for the day he can get on with his life and back to his loved ones. He suffers daily both mentally and physically. It's a double-edged sword! This suffering has been a suffering of thousands of days and a suffering sure to continue for thousands more.

Poetry | *Maria Rouphail*

WHAT YOU WANT TO SAY

———

(in 2022)

Here is not where you died.
Neither this room,
nor a hospital intensive care unit
was your final living whereabouts.
No priest was summoned
to anoint your hands and feet.
Your kin did not sit vigil at a computer terminal,
nor friends weep into their cell phones.
As for the liminal space between worlds,
you gave no account, for you did not enter or return from it.

What then,
for as long as there is time,
but to love the wind moving
in the backyard beech like a holy spirit.
It rickles through the screens, bathing your face.
And the sun splayed on these walls
which your own hands painted "Antique Jade,"
the white ginger jar lamps, the dresser
with the black lacquer jewelry box inlaid with abalone.
The votive candle,

and the gilt icon
your grandmother and mother passed on,
which they'd carried into every place they and you lived.
Before it they taught you how to pray.
On days of pain and joy, you lit a flame
and sang to the Mother of God.

ZOOM FUNERAL

We appear in little squares—
a sheet of commemorative stamps,
minus the commemorated one;
four generations—all over the map—together,
sans hugs, food, schmooze.

Newspapers and the radio
echo our words—at the end
we weren't there for her. I repeat those words
till they belong more to history than to me.
We'd have been endangered, a danger.

Regaled with tales from my mother's life,
we view photos of her art,
snapshots of her over the years:
Her life flashes before my eyes
as if I were dying.

Music brings mute sobs.
I square my shaking shoulders.
The song ends. Composed,
I smile at my family, then
our windows blacken.

Previously published in *Poetry and Covid*

FOR JON, WHO DIED BECAUSE OF TIME

———

I.
I was thinking of you the other day,
could picture the contours of your face,
paint the tone of your skin,
sketch that unmistakable beard
and the look you give, contemplative.

Turns out, you had already passed.

I didn't know at first,
because you died in a prison
and in this pandemic
the keepers make it harder
to stay in touch.

Call it impossible,
more impossible than it already was
to check in on loved ones in cages
and make sure they're ok,

whatever that means.

II.
I thought of my friend while he was
already gone a week, I am told,
through an email from a dear friend

who heard through an email from an acquaintance,
because a mutual friend asked her
to get the bleak news outside.

The thought of Swiss Army Craig
and whether he cried or wept
or is crying or weeping,
or giving a sermon like he does,
with Jon on mind, his wife on mind,
his mother on mind.

The thought of Mikey
barely able to stand with his grief,
and the eight other men in that penitentiary
that changed me moments after meeting,
how I can't bear to sit
with their loss
locked in those concrete tombs.

III.
And there's no way
to make him undead so I can
say all the things,
so he knows how much
he was thought of and loved.

That I sit with his poems and
ponder what he calls "weeding the garden,"
the sifting of words until
they land on the page *just right*,

and wonder if wherever he is,
he is still weeding.

As I curse the prison industrial complex
that leaves humans to die before
their time, while
doing time, because
of time.

SURVIVAL: *Remember every surface you touch*

"CONFINED," PHOTOGRAPH · JUDEA COSTES, 2022

Poetry | *Katy Giebenhain*

ESSENTIAL NONESSENTIALS IN LOCKDOWN

You're okay if you don't bake,
if you didn't get a dog from the shelter,
if you didn't get a cat from the shelter, if you haven't invented
a margarita named after your street.
You're okay if you've never seen sourdough starter
or the inside of an Instant Pot.

You're okay if you don't knit,
if you're not doing sit-ups like Batman in prison,
or aerobics in the dining room with soup cans for weights.
You're okay if you're not on Instagram,
if you don't work in a hospital or nursing home.
If you have or have not been to college.

You're okay if you don't teach,
if you haven't taken your violin out
of the closet for decades, if you don't have kids or a kit
to grow herbs indoors. You're okay if you don't
have Netflix, are afraid to cut your own hair
or if you don't vacuum each room with the crevice tool.

You're okay if you don't pray,
if you want to pray, if you used to pray, if you feel lame
about not praying, if you have no interest in praying.
You're okay if you do. You're okay if you miss
airport cappuccinos and if you feel bad or good or just tired.
You are. You are. You are.

THE EATERS

———

"And then we'll take a right when we pass the large maple tree," he said.

Shelby suppressed a sigh. He's gonna kill us, she thought.

Terrance had been back around for less than a week and with it, he brought his usual chaos. Even in the middle of an apocalyptic event, even as death stood tall and proud on his doorstep, his fear got the best of him and he was scattered, defensive even. He couldn't help himself.

But not everything was the same. Two months alone in the middle of nowhere had made Shelby sharp and agile. She wasn't the same woman.

"Babe, if we go left we'll pass by a freshwater stream. Ground was wet when we were back there hunting."

A long silence passed as he swallowed.

"Quicker this wa—,"

"It's not. I know these woods well," she said.

He laughed, his face hard.

"Seriously, we can probably save at least two miles. Cut around the tree and make a right at the abandoned hiking trail. Once we get on that we'll meet the coast in no time."

"Why do we need fresh water anyway?" he asked.

"We gotta leave all our stuff. Won't make it in time with all of the bags," she said.

Terrence chortled. She sighed aloud this time.

"I ain't leaving my bag. No protection."

"If we want to get there in time there's no choice." Her words were sharp, tiny little daggers that caused him to poke out his chest even more.

"We'll take your route, but the bag is coming."

"That bag will be the death of us," she said quietly. Terrence looked past her, out into the distance.

She was right and they both knew it, still his resentment hung thick in the air. Shelby watched as he rubbed his brow. She thought about a time before all of this.

Four years ago, when they first fell in love, she'd make him dinner every night. He'd walk through the door with a big smile on his face and pull her into his arms, kissing her.

In the mornings she'd make him breakfast and watch him go to work. When he left she'd close her eyes and inhale his lingering cologne—missing him already.

And from those small moments grew a life. There were fights and sex—frustrations and vacations. Laughter filled the home but resentment crept in too, like a cancer.

He was a beautiful but broken spirit. He knew loss intimately and there was a loneliness to him, always lurking just under the surface. But his arms felt like her home and when life knocked her about he was there. Her solace in a storm.

But sometimes, he'd block the whole world out. The walls of his castle came up and the tiny army ferociously guarded the King. There was no getting in. There was no getting close.

A few months ago, just when she'd found enough strength to declare she needed more and summoned up enough courage to start anew, disaster hit.

It started on a Wednesday in Seattle, with a few dead bodies turning up in the woods back by Green Lake. Cops thought it was a coyote attack, until the bloody mess at the gas station. A customer walked in and found an associate and four people with their faces ripped off, limbs missing. Then word came about the Eaters down in Texas.

By the time authorities realized that they had to burn the bodies, that after twenty-four hours they became Eaters, it was too late. Twelve Eaters broke out of the county morgue and feasted on fifty people. Those fifty Eaters turned into a hundred and all too soon life was turned upside down.

No one knows how it started, though there's a million different theories. Shelby figured it didn't matter much how they got there as much as it mattered how they'd get out.

After about three months of uncertainty, Terrence told her it was time to go. There was a boat in California waiting to take them to shelter, he said. The dock was remote and could only be accessed through the coastal Algonquin Trail. He told her the journey would take about two months, give or take, and to pack the necessities.

She had no time to think, no time to object, no time to plan. Terrence snapped his fingers and they left.

It took them thirteen hours to drive from Washington to Northern California. She watched from her window as the rain slowly turned to fog, inhaling and exhaling fear and uncertainty along the way.

The Algonquin Trail was once a vibrant and bustling city named Lindy. After the riots and fires, the city was evacuated and no one ever came back. Now it was a dangerous tangle of trees and overgrown plants, though there were some signs of life at the edge of the city. There was an abandoned school and a library, even a few summer cabins scattered about, but deep into the trail the pathways were narrow, if they existed at all, and the ground was slippery.

The forest reminded her of a maze. Weeds and roots grew up and devoured paths. Clear pathways went on for hours before ending abruptly, suddenly leaving hikers lost in the middle of the dense forest.

Slowly, and much to Shelby's horror, she realized Terrence had no clue what he was doing. After two months they were no closer to the coast than when they began. Tired of eating plants and potentially poisonous berries, she began hunting and cooking. Tired of being lost, she studied the map and learned the tangled and unforgiving trail. But when it came time to give her input on the plan—the real plan that concerned her life as much as it did hers—Terrence would hear none of it.

One day, low on food and hot and tired, they began to argue over where to rest. Terrence was convinced the abandoned library was safe. He'd forgotten about how the Eaters had attacked a family there just last week. Shelby hadn't. She heard the story on her favorite radio show. Came on every Wednesday—depending on the connection.

"Welcome to the Run Radio. Sad news today, as Eaters have taken the lives of what appears to be a family of four last night. They were hiding out in the Monroe County Public Library. We have reason to believe that Eaters were alerted to the family's presence when a bathroom light was left on. No word on whether or not the bodies were burned. This story is still developing."

Shelby listened with her headphones in and rushed to tell Terrence who was clumsily trying to start a fire.

"It's going to be fine," he said, but his eyes were blank. Some days she wondered if he'd digested the seriousness of the moment or if it was the seriousness which was too much for him. Either way, she had no time for it. Eaters were roaming that library freely, she was sure of it.

"I'm not going there," she said.

The stick snapped in his hands and he threw the lighter down.

"I can't do this," he said. "I can't."

Her heart dropped.

"Go wherever you want Shelb, but I'm going to the library."

"What? What does that mean?"

"It means I can't do this with you," he said.

She knew he was afraid. He was the most fearful man she'd ever met, and she knew when he was scared he ran.

But a funny thing happened in that moment. For the first time in a long time she had no desire to chase him.

So she watched as he walked away, kicking up dirt every step of the way.

Two months. That's how long she was there alone. The first night was the hardest. She hiked northeast, far away from the abandoned library. When dusk came, she hid underneath the log of a dead tree, the needles pricked her skin as she cried. She was sure the Eaters would find her, but they never came. Just before she dozed off she thought of Terrance. She wondered if he was safe. She missed his arms around hers, protecting her as best as he could.

The days rambled on and on, eventually becoming longer. Plants burst from their stems and wildlife began to awaken. Shelby became a skilled hunter, rising early to catch her meals for the day, hiking through the tangled forest toward the coast, and feasting on squirrel or rabbit every night. Her life went on like that; resting under a rock or in a cave for a few days, then back through the trees to hunt. Her radio kept her connected and once a week she'd tune in for new routes and Eater updates.

In the middle of an abandoned forest, cold and lonely, Shelby was happy. It was the happiest she'd been in years. But on nights where she couldn't fall asleep, she'd lie awake thinking of Terrence. She thought of how, on a hot summer night with the moon lighting the way, they snuck onto the beach and danced by the ocean. His smile was bright and his laughter was deep and sincere. He wrapped her into his arms and she inhaled his scent. In that moment her heart swelled with love. This, she thought, is home.

That night Shelby didn't cry, she simply tucked the memory away with the swift hand of the truth. Terrence was gone. He would not be coming back.

About six weeks later she saw the marker. A large red X painted on the side of a tree. She leaped for joy. According to her map—which she no longer needed, as she was now well acquainted with the trail—she was only ten miles away. Shelby Harris had done the impossible.

She decided to rest for the night, right next to the tree with the large X on it. Normally she would camp near water but today she was too tired.

Tomorrow she'd get up early, wash up, and head out. She was close.

But in the middle of the night a painful groan woke her. Her stomach immediately dropped. They're here, she thought. Before she could reach for her knife, an Eater grabbed her by the throat.

She looked him in the eyes, rotten skin covered his dull and lifeless face and just as he went to sink a big bite into Shelby's neck someone attacked him from behind. He folded, dropping Shelby in the process.

"Get back," Terrence said.

And quite miraculously, she watched him move quickly to douse the Eater with gasoline and set him on fire.

Terrence saved the day. Deep in Shelby's heart, where there should have been gratefulness, there was only resentment.

"Thanks," she said. He reached for her, enveloping her into a tight hug.

"I missed you," he whispered.

It only took me nearly dying, she thought.

There was no discussion about his departure. The next day when Shelby tried to bring it up Terrence looked away and with tears in his eyes uttered just a few words.

"You didn't make it easy."

Her eyes narrowed. Typical. Even with death staring him in the face, even after abandoning her, this would be the extent of his atonement. She shook her head ever so slightly. A week later and here they were, close to freedom and further from each other than ever before.

They hiked for a day or two, with Shelby leading the way and Terrence's suggestions falling flat.

Finally, when Terrence declared he couldn't possibly go on without a rest, they stopped at an abandoned cabin and decided to camp for the day. They would make their final descent tomorrow and Shelby couldn't wait. She yearned for freedom, a safe space to cry and grieve. Shelby needed a place to lick her wounds and build anew.

Terrence also had plans. Plans to marry Shelby like she'd always wanted. Plans to give her babies and create a family together. If they could survive this, they could survive anything, he told her. She smiled, not having the heart or the courage to tell him that she no longer wanted to have his babies. In fact, she no longer wanted him around. She missed the days when they were young and naive enough to think it could work. The days when they were inexperienced enough to love each other fully; those days shined bright in her mind. The memories were glorious, but it wasn't enough to compete with reality.

She tried not to be so hard on him. She reminded herself daily that she loved him for a reason. But now she could not seem to find it. There had been too many betrayals. Too much pleading and not enough loving turned her heart sour.

As they cooked their lunch, squirrel that Shelby had hunted, he smiled at her.

"We're gonna get through this Shelb," he said. "And we'll be better than ever."

She looked at him and remembered the boy with the big smile. She remembered how every Sunday he'd pull the covers off of her, exposing her body to the cold, wrap her tight in his arms and stroke her hair. She felt the warmth of his spirit on those days—though it never lasted long.

That night they went to sleep just before dusk, lighting a fire to keep the Eaters away.

The seven-mile hike to shore took longer than Shelby realized. The path was a dangerous one, uphill with steep cliffs overlooking jagged rocks and sharp turns. There was no shade, so the sun beamed down on them the entire journey.

Terrence's bag slowed them down as well, but Shelby didn't dare mention it. The black bag was heavy and though it contained water, blankets, and other necessities, one sharp turn and the weight of the bag could send him hurling over a cliff. So he moved slowly, carefully.

Just as dusk arrived, the coastline came into view. Shelby beamed. Then reality set in. They were about one hour away. But darkness would come sooner.

"We need to pick up the pace," she said. "We can't camp out here, there's nowhere to hide."

"I'm trying," he said. Shelby stopped walking, giving him a chance to catch up. He met her and handed her his water bottle. As she gulped the water down, a rustling from the bushes sent chills down her back.

"Let's go," she said. The Eaters were beginning to wake and she didn't know how many lived on this mountain. She hoped only a few.

The sun was setting rapidly now, and the coastline was in plain sight. In the distance Shelby thought she saw a boat.

She looked behind her and saw Terrence struggling to keep up. The weight on his shoulders was too heavy. She wanted to yell, "Take off that backpack!" But something stopped her.

They were walking fast now, hopping over branches and climbing down slippery rocks.

A painful groan came from behind Shelby. Her breath caught in her throat. She turned around to find three Eaters lazily walking toward them.

"Run," Terrence cried out as he grabbed her hand. They sped across bushes and slid down more rocks. Still the groans grew closer. Shelby felt herself slowing down to meet Terrence, slowing down to meet the Eaters too.

"Hurry," she said. Up ahead there was a fork in the road, slick from rain. "We're going left," she said. At the turn Terrence fell, and her hand slipped from his.

She stopped and turned just in time to see the Eaters overtake him.

"Go!" he screamed as he tried in vain to reach for the gasoline in his bag. At the coastline a horn sounded three times. The boat had docked. She didn't have much time. And so she turned back around and ran. She ran until his screams and their groans faded to black. She ran until the Eaters were nothing more than a memory. She ran until Terrence was too.

She made it to the coastline and swam to the boat. Inside it was warm and safe. After she'd showered and told her story a million times, she went to her room, closed the door, and cried.

Finally, she was alone.

OFF-SCRIPT

———————

Contact tracing called, they want my condolences
every call I make is a punch to my ear,
strong enough to knock my heart into the depths of my stomach
I dragged Sympathy along
She asked if we were done yet
I wish she behaved like her sister Empathy
You have been identified as a close contact of a COVID-19 case

The unbelievers yell obscenities in my direction
They refuse to believe the "unbelievable"
They pray to a savior whose "crucifixion" was his impeachment
Even then, they don't turn to God

I was asked if the pandemic is real
As real as my beating heart, I say
As real as the coughing fits I get when overexerted
At this time, we recommend that you begin your quarantine period

I've been cried at
How could I have been so cruel? they stammer
When a father cried in anger
I listened
I collect the tears in a jar next to my window
I let them marinate in the moonlight
in hopes that maybe the universe will listen

A woman contemplated her mortality
I was the bungee cord she latched onto
I became her noose and her salvation
If I hung up
She wouldn't be here
During this time, please stay at home and monitor your symptoms

I asked for their closest contacts
They close up claiming they saw no one
Their trauma response is to lie

Contact Tracing called . . . they wanted to stay objective
When religion is more prosperous than cicadas in a southern
    summer
How can you stay objective?

Lessons unlearned based on a notion of freedom
Then we curse each other when confined to an oxygen tank
We will now as a series of questions, this should take no longer
    than 10 minutes

the pandemic wears death as a crown,
as she makes demands for her daily quota to be filled
Group gatherings are her happy place
And the exposed faces of the unmasked
gave her anonymity
We are collecting critical information that can help stop the spread of
    COVID-19 within our community

The vaccinated cry in vehement vociferation
Becoming moralized at the immortalization of others
They are the "unhinged" probing the uncharted

The hypocrisy that dwells in our society
Laughs at the hole we've dug ourselves in
When playing God is no longer recreational
But a race against a microscopic parasite that clings to our weak-
    est links

HEROES

––––––––

The virus had ripped through two nursing homes in our small city like a poisonous tornado, killing sixteen residents. Three churches and one high school gym had been the sites of super-spreader events. People returning from spring vacations at crowded beaches brought home not only sand in their shoes but death on their breath. We, the citizens of Sherman, Ohio, looked warily at each other like players in a game of Wink Murder. Silent killers were everywhere.

When Toby and I sat on a metal bench in what we called the Hanger, where Food World's broken grocery carts were stored, we had a panoramic view of the parking lot and could track the comings and goings of the store's customers. We pretended we weren't working stiffs—I bagged groceries, Toby managed the produce department—but infectious disease specialists who could diagnose a person from a hundred feet. "That man in the blue shirt? Infected." "The woman who just stepped out of the silver Volvo? Yep." "That whole sunburned family caught the plague along with the waves at Daytona Beach." We inevitably spared the old ladies who shuffled past us, their masks covering all but their weary and wary eyes, from our devastating diagnoses.

Before long, we didn't only assess who had the virus but what the virus would do to the infected. Inevitably, middle-aged men who stepped out of their pickups with puffed-up self-regard and macho disdain for masks were, in Toby's eyes, doomed. "Dead man shopping," Toby would proclaim. "Dead, dead, dead."

Sometimes I'd point to girls who reminded me of my ex-girlfriend. Samantha dumped me after I made out with her best friend at a New Year's Eve party, back when parties didn't have pathogens on their guest lists. I couldn't forgive her for not forgiving me. Even more unforgiveable:

two weeks after our breakup, she started dating a tall, blond lacrosse player named Leif who, no joke, called himself Leif Erikson, like the explorer. Although well within my wounded ego's right to do so, I didn't have the heart to forecast death upon her lookalikes. "She'll have a fever for three days," I said about one. "She'll be asymptomatic during the day, but at night she'll keep the whole neighborhood awake with her coughing and feverish, delirious opera singing," I said about another. And my direst prediction: "She'll have trouble breathing, but she'll survive with the help of supplemental oxygen while her asshole of a boyfriend, who gave her the virus, will die on a Viking ship bound for his native Greenland."

The parking lot was a kind of graveyard, and we were witnesses to the living dead.

I was seventeen and about to start my senior year in high school. Toby was twenty-three and had been working at Food World since his first and only year at college. In February of his spring semester, he'd been busted for weed possession, and his father, ex-military, told him if he was stupid enough to break the law, he was too stupid to go to college. He stopped paying Toby's tuition and threatened to hire a collection agency to recover what he'd blown on his son's fall semester. Toby figured he'd work at Food World for a year or two, then go back to school on his own dime. Five years later, he had saved enough money for a semester and a half, providing he ate absolutely nothing and stole his textbooks. He had no interest in student loans. Some of his friends who'd graduated from college were thousands of dollars in debt and had jobs only half as good as his.

Toby claimed to be one-eighth Native American on his mother's side, but he looked stereotypical Irish to me: pale skin with orange freckles, curly orange hair, and an orange-brown goatee that he was so proud of he'd given it a name: the Captain. I was taller and thinner than Toby, and my skin was darker because of my Nicaraguan mother, a state of affairs that had prompted one of my geographically challenged classmates the past school year to recommend, loudly, that I "Go back to Mexico." Toby and I wore the same blue-and-orange Food World uniform with nametags that identified us, in the company's official lingo, as "associates," although Toby preferred to think of the two of us as bandmates and the workday as one long blues song.

My Food World gig was only a summer job. I didn't need the money. My parents were accountants, and they not only knew how to pinch a penny but how to strangle it. They'd started saving for my college education when I was a zygote, and they had their hearts, and their bank accounts, set on the Ivy League. They were, however, eager to see me prove I had an acceptable work ethic after I'd spent every day of the previous summer on and around the diving board at the Sky Lake Community Pool, doing cannonballs and jackknives and flying squirrels with the hope of impressing a pink-haired, bored lifeguard named Wendy Wilde. When it was obvious I wasn't going to impress her, I aimed to impress the twelve-year-old boys who inevitably lined up behind me. I had no better luck with them, the brats.

It was company policy for employees, as well as customers, to wear masks inside the store. Toby and I wore them in the Hanger, too. Toby had asthma, which made him more vulnerable to a severe reaction to the virus than most people, and the previous winter, he'd moved in with his grandmother, his mother's mother, so he could look after her. He didn't want to come home to her one evening with a bag full of groceries and a mouth full of morbidity. He had no choice but to work, however, and as he stocked the avocado bin or refilled shelves with clam-shell containers of blueberries and strawberries, customers would sometimes approach him unmasked and breathe questions into his face. He believed he was destined to catch the virus—"A question of *when*, not *if*," he said—although pessimism had always been part of his portfolio, he admitted. In high school, he was in a band called the Doomed Damned. As its lyricist, he wrote melancholy odes to melting icebergs and bleached coral reefs. He was planning to study poetry in college, which was another reason his father was reluctant to pay his way. "Poet isn't a profession," his father said. "It's a lifestyle choice."

One morning, Toby told me about a woman who'd approached him as he was unloading a crate of gala apples. She stopped her cart six feet from him, excused herself for interrupting his work, and said, "I just want to tell you I appreciate your heroism. You're on the frontline, and you're feeding us all." His first instinct was to laugh and set her straight: If he were offered a higher paying job that put him in contact with zero people—and even fewer apples, Brussels sprouts, and cantaloupes—he would accept it in a heartbeat. His second thought was about his father, who'd fought in the first Gulf War and let his two sons know about it frequently. "The difference between courage and cowardice," his father said once, "is whether you hold your ground or turn ass and run." Toby asked his father—playfully—whether it counted as courage if you were so scared you couldn't move and therefore succeeded in holding your ground. "I was hoping he would say, 'Sure, as long as you don't shit your pants,'" Toby said. But his father gave him a disappointed scowl and a don't-be-a-wise-ass lecture. Toby's brother, two years older, followed their father's life path: GED, the army, Iraq. He had an additional item on his military resume: PTSD.

I didn't know what to say to the lady besides "thank you" and "you've made a great choice with that organic Rotisserie chicken," Toby said. "Soon enough, she was heading down the bread aisle—in accordance with the one-way arrow, of course—and thanking Old Ted, who was stuffing the shelves with hamburger buns, for his selfless service to the nation."

I'd never thought of my job at Food World as heroic. Now that I knew that at least one person believed so, I decided to play the part. Standing at the end of the conveyor belt in aisle 6, I squared my shoulders and, gazing at the magazines on the racks beyond the register, pictured myself defending the country from disgraced British royalty and pregnant Hollywood stars. To departing customers, I sometimes followed my "have a nice day" with "God bless America."

———

"That dude," Toby said one afternoon in July. He pointed to a beefy bald man in a tight olive drab T-shirt and black slacks who'd parked his pickup at the far edge of the Food World lot. "He breathed in a super dose of the virus when he was working out at his illegally opened gym, and in three days, he'll be on a ventilator, wishing he'd never met a dumbbell or a Nautilus machine."

As the man drew closer to the store's entrance, Toby said, "Oops."

"What?" I said.

"That's my dad."

The man strode into the store through the out entrance, nearly colliding with one of our favorite old ladies. He wasn't wearing a mask. "I just killed him off, didn't I, with my words?" Toby said. "Like the Food World incarnation of Oedipus."

"Are you going to say hello to him?" I asked.

"I'm not wearing the right uniform." He patted his orange-and-blue Food World outfit. "Only when I get a few bars on my shoulders is he likely to talk to me again."

"Does he know you work here?"

"Sure," Toby said.

"Maybe," I said, smiling, "he's coming to thank you for your service."

"I'm just glad I'm not working at the moment. He'd want to restart whatever argument we hadn't finished five years ago."

A few minutes later, Toby's father left the store, holding a carton of Marlboros, and walked to his truck without so much as a glance around the lot. As he drove off, I said, "Sorry, man."

"He isn't a total asshole," Toby said. "When I was in sixth grade, he taught me how to throw a Frisbee."

I thought there might be more to the story, so I waited. Finally, I said, "Yeah?"

"Yeah. Because of him, I can throw a Frisbee. Pretty straight too."

"Oh. Okay."

"And because of him, I damn sure know how to salute." He snapped me a salute like a cadet at the top of his West Point class.

———

Three days later, my parents insisted that I quit my job. They'd heard a report on NPR that our small city had become a hot spot in a state that was already a hot spot. They didn't want me to put myself any longer in what my father called "harm's way." My new summer job, they said, would be to help around the house. In the end, this consisted of two tasks: mowing the lawn and brushing our two Persian cats. I didn't think either duty would look impressive on my résumé, especially because I skimped on the cat brushing. I spent most of my time reading horror novels and playing video games. I didn't miss my job, but I missed Toby, even if ours wasn't a friendship that had ever been likely to continue outside the Hanger. I didn't even have his cell phone number.

Before long, though, I did reach him by phone—the one next to his bed at University Hospital. Two weeks after I quit, he was shot during a dispute in Food World. The story was front-page news in our small city's small newspaper—and it did a few circles around the internet as well. The shooter was a forty-six-year-old unemployed bartender named Ryan Allen. According to the newspaper, the unmasked Allen strode over to the banana bin and ploughed into a seventy-six-year-old woman who was reaching for the last unbruised bunch. Toby raced over from tomatoes to remind Allen of Food World's mask-wearing and social-distancing policies. Witnesses reported hearing Allen call Toby a socialist and a fascist. Toby—politely, by all accounts—pointed out that the two political philosophies tended to be mutually exclusive. The disturbed former bartender whipped out a pistol and fired twice. The first bullet whizzed past Toby and struck an artichoke "in the heart," as the newspaper faithfully reported. The second struck Toby in the right shoulder. Allen was apprehended in the parking lot. He was charged with attempted manslaughter and shoplifting. He'd left the store with five bananas.

I didn't talk to Toby for long on the phone. He was pumped up with painkillers, he said, and they either made him want to sleep or write psychedelic song lyrics. I told him I'd catch up with him at Food World when he was well enough to return. Thankfully, he was healing faster than the doctors expected—a good thing, he said, for both himself and the hospital, which needed his bed for the next COVID patient. Our small city's medical facilities continued to fill with the infected.

A month and a half after I'd last seen him, I visited Toby in the Hanger. I felt naked without my Food World uniform. His, meanwhile, looked two sizes too large; he must have lost fifteen pounds since the shooting. He welcomed me like old times, though we didn't play our usual game of guessing who had the virus. Things had turned too serious. Or maybe they'd crossed over from the serious into the absurd. Toby said he'd received dozens of letters, emails, and phone calls from around the world. Some were from firearm fanatics who accused him of provoking the shooting in order to give ammunition, as it were, to the anti-gun crowd. On the flip side, the elderly woman he'd attempted to spare from Ryan Allen's deadly breath had started a GoFundMe campaign to raise money for his college tuition. Food World had promised to match the amount up to $25,000 as long as he identified himself in any future media as a "Food World Scholar."

Toby said our newspaper's headline writers had missed a golden opportunity with its story about the shooting. "They should have gone with some variation of 'Armed Man Goes Bananas in Fruit Aisle,'" he said.

I pointed to the squiggly black lines on his white mask, and he said, "I didn't have a cast for anyone to autograph, so I had my nurses sign one of my masks. I felt like a kid at a baseball game, holding out a Sharpie to All-Stars. What you hear is true: they're total heroes."

"You're a hero yourself," I said.

"For getting shot?" He laughed. "My dad did come see me the day I came home. Brought his purple heart and placed it on my chest. I thought he was joking. I was ready to play along, say something like, 'Yeah, you think the Battle of the Bulge was ferocious? You haven't seen combat until you step into a firefight at Food World.' But, no, like always, he was serious—so serious he started crying. I thought he might be remembering some of his own trauma, and maybe he was, but he kept saying, 'I'll do better, son. I'll do better.'"

"Has he?"

"I talk to him every day now. I have to make shit up sometimes to keep the conversation going. There's only so much to talk about when life these days is dedicated principally to the boring quest of avoiding the virus."

"So far, so good."

"Yeah, I guess," he said. "It isn't fair, though. Getting shot should have given me immunity to the virus. It doesn't even give me immunity to being shot again."

We talked a little more, and then it was time for him to go back to work. We stood up; social distancing meant we wouldn't shake hands. After saying goodbye, I gave him a little wave, my right hand fluttering near my right eyebrow. He shot back a crisp salute. "Carry on," he said, and we did.

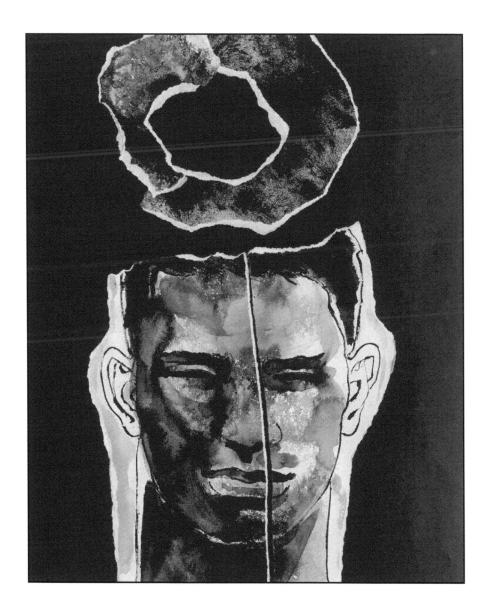

"MAN IMAGINES," WATERCOLOR · RICHARD VYSE, 2020

Poetry | *Peter Joel*

15 MAR 2020—A ROLL IN THE HAND IS WORTH TWO ON THE SHELF

———

The me-first movement
Use their hoarded toilet rolls
For rear-guard actions

Poetry | *Blessing Omeiza Ojo*

WE WILL SING OF GONE BODIES SOME DAYS FROM NOW

———

after the news of a man beaten to death by a Nigerian
policeman in Abuja for violating COVID -19 lock down

What you don't know about songs is that the lyrics
of a new song live in the things we behold and hear.
A second look at an ant hiding its head beneath
the earth exposes the number of its legs and thorax.
I do not doubt you've wondered what the armed man
who lives in your neighborhood does as work until
the news of a tiny invisible broom sweeping the streets
of our globe, of dirt we never knew we had. The police
man who lives in my compound told his wife he won't
come home until after 14 days. And I prayed silently.
Everything has a class here. I belong to the one with
feeble frames. You heard what the sailor said a few days
ago. There was a storm here. What happens over there?
On that day, I searched everywhere for a song to chew
perhaps to seal my mouth of storms. There was none
because I didn't shake well the mixture of roots, barks,
and liquor newly served to us, for fear of being drunk
and it could drive me to call upon waters to have a taste
of the sailor's flesh, you know. Of what use is a body
dead to stimulus? To say you're a human is to wear the
skin of a childless widow who awaits the break of dawn
to recharge her cell daily, is to cease your breath,

to be a stagnant water, to know the stenches a steady
body consumes. Some days from now, we will sing
of misted bodies shown the way to another habitat by men,
our supposed shield. And the chorus would be: this is
an addendum to those burnt by herders, to the ones given
a holy death by boko brothers, to those blown into light
particles for air to carry into places beyond us.

IN TIMES OF QUARANTINE

———

Buy dried beans and rice.
Try to find hand sanitizer and bleach.
Make friends with someone crafty
who will sew you a cloth mask
and leave it in your mailbox.

Tie your hair up before you go outside.
Remember every surface you touch.
Hit the crosswalk button with a high kick
your kickboxing instructor would be proud of.

Shrink your world to your walls,
your garden, your neighborhood park.
Retract. Go inward.
Count your blessings:
We don't have to breathe the same air
to see the faces we love.

Everyone is now the exact same distance away.

HALMONI'S KIMCHI PANCAKES

———————

Growing up as a Korean American, I was always shy about sharing my culture. I bought clothes, talked, and mimicked the white people in elementary school. I was not ashamed of being Korean, but I felt a gravitation toward mushing down my heritage. Through the hardships of "fitting in," I found comfort in eating Korean food privately. My favorite dish my *halmoni*, or grandmother, made was kimchi pancakes. My halmoni and I shared a passion for cooking because of the warmth it brought to our family. I began to adore my Korean culture through high school, but then the coronavirus hit. While visiting Wyoming, I couldn't help but feel watched. The normalized racism toward the Asian community dramatically intensified, and I was transported to being a fifth grader again. I found myself staying inside and eating kimchi pancakes from March through May. My halmoni's pancakes have been a reminder of my Korean heritage through this pandemic and will always be a source of gentle support. I offer this recipe so others can find the same comfort in this impossible time.

2 cups fermented kimchi
½ yellow onion
2 serrano peppers
½ tbsp sugar
1 ⅔ cups ice cold water
1 cup Korean pancake mix
1 cup Korean frying batter mix
A splash of kimchi juice (optional)
Cooking oil

1. Chop the kimchi and thinly slice the onion. Place them into a large bowl.
2. Finely chop the serrano peppers and add them to the bowl.
3. Add the sugar, pancake mix, frying mix, and cold water to the bowl. Gently toss the batter until there are no clumps (do not overmix!). The mixture should look slightly thin and watery.
4. Depending on the kimchi used, the batter can vary in saltiness. If the kimchi is not very sour, add a splash of kimchi juice to balance out the flavor.
5. Place a frying pan on high to heat. Add a generous amount of cooking oil and lower the temperature to medium heat. Spread the batter thinly.
6. Twirl the pancake around the pan while adding oil to the edges if it seems dry.
7. When the edges start to cook, flip the pancake and continue to twirl it.
8. Once well cooked, flip the pancake again, and serve. The ideal pancake is crispy and golden brown. Enjoy!

Note: If the batter is too thick, add more ice water and be sure to cook the pancake with a generous amount of oil. If the batter is too thin, add the dry mixes in equal amounts.

COVID CURRICULUM

———

For teacher licensure renewal and personal interest, I decided to enroll in a graduate certificate program in Appalachian Studies. On a Thursday night, I cleared a few Facebook notifications, scrolled through Pinterest while my five-year-old took his bath, and finished the assigned reading for the week. I underlined a section of the text that stated, "[teacher] burnout based on 'structural strain,' or the idea that when societies and the institutions within them change too rapidly, individuals within the institutions find it impossible to cope" (LeCompte and Schensul 21). *Sad, but true*, I thought. In my district, teacher turnover rates are high, while salaries are painstakingly low. A first year teacher with a bachelor's degree, according to the district 2020–21 salary scale, makes $33,000. County poverty is rampant at 20 percent, literally double the Virginia State average (Census.gov). Some four-wheel drive vehicles struggle to traverse our hollers and mountains, so internet access to many students is a pipe dream. And they are not alone. Based on pre-pandemic census data, the NEA recently reported that one quarter of US households with children ages five to seventeen lacked either high-speed internet, a computer, or both. For households near the poverty line, the number was closer to half. So these "structural strains" and I were already well acquainted. My mind harped on these issues until I fell asleep. It was March 12. Little did I know, my focus should have been on how institutions "change too rapidly."

Much like the events of 9/11, I will remember exactly where I was and what I was doing when our governor shut down schools for the initial two weeks during the COVID-19 pandemic. I was in the Woodlands High School library with my friend and colleague, Missy, and three students, all seniors, rehearsing their forensics pieces for the upcoming Virginia High School League State Competition. Kenzie, slated to be a repeat state champion and Missy's daughter, had just finished her piece—a hysterical children's tale about a penguin trying out for the cheer team—when Alli held up her phone and said, "Uh, is this real?" She had just received a text from a friend that said, "Schools are shutting down!" Before Missy or I could respond, our own phones erupted in an ensemble of ringtones. I opened my first message, a notification from WCYB (the local news station). The governor had, in fact, publicly announced at 2:45 p.m. that he would be closing schools for two weeks in an effort to "flatten the curve" of the novel coronavirus. I looked at the clock. It was 3:01 p.m.

By 3:02 p.m. the hallways were overrun with panicked students. Several came into the library, the underclassmen excited, the seniors sobbing. Jen, a quirky and compassionate senior, burst into the library and fell into my arms. "It's over, isn't it? We're never coming back, are we? Are we?" She was inconsolable. She was one of many. I held Jen, Kenzie, and Alli. All I could do was utter, "It's not time to worry"—a line lifted from Atticus Finch. The principal stepped into the library with the assistant principal directly behind him. "We didn't know about this. Nobody knew about this!" they said in near unison. Then, they were gone as quickly as they had arrived, and a few seconds later an announcement erupted over the loudspeaker. What was said, I still am not sure. Buses lined up outside. Student after student asked question after question. I had no answers. Missy had no answers. None of us did. Then another announcement, this one I managed to understand. "Faculty meeting immediately after school!" Our principal tried to convey what the assistant superintendent was telling him over the phone. The assistant principal was relaying messages from his phone, too. *Virtual for two weeks. Chromebooks. Packets when necessary.* Little was known by 3:17 p.m. on Friday, March 13.

Adapt and overcome, be flexible, meet them where they are. All things that thirteen years in the public school classroom taught me. I had also been teaching asynchronously for years with various institutions, so *I could do this*, I thought, sitting in my usual spot during the faculty meeting. A little time, a little tweaking here and there, and I could do this. But then, as I looked around the room surveying the faces of my coworkers, my eyes found Aaron, a first-year English teacher and coach. There was a look of total shock on his face. Aaron, the compact muscle machine with no neck who coached our linemen, was sweating profusely, wide-eyed, and horrified. I don't think the man had ever been scared before in his life. We were instructed to spend the weekend preparing what we could do, anticipating what we might have to do, and waiting for more information. We would have another faculty meeting first thing Monday.

Monday morning, I filed out of the meeting behind Aaron. He was still sweating. Had he even stopped since Friday? I entered my classroom and started moving two weeks' worth of *To Kill a Mockingbird* material to my Google Classroom. At some point between Dill running away and Scout's "Po-ork!" cue, I headed to the office lounge for coffee. I had to pass by the copier to get to the caffeine, and it just so happened that an unraveling Aaron was white-knuckling both sides of the industrial-sized copier. He dwarfed the machine. In my own haste, I had not even thought to check on him, despite witnessing him dehydrating right before my eyes on multiple occasions. I looked at him. His complexion was an odd blend of pinks, reds, and whites. I stopped. "Can I help?" He didn't lift his head. He didn't loosen his hands. "Four years for a bachelor's and two years for a master's. Six years of college. Nothing prepared me for this." Statistics presented by Abigail Johnson Hess of CNBC.com revealed that "77% of educators are working more today than a year ago, 60% enjoy their job less and 59% do not feel secure in their school district's health and safety precautions. Roughly 27% say they are considering leaving their job, retiring early or taking a leave of absence because of the pandemic." Aaron walked out of the office and then the building that afternoon. Would he confirm these statistics?

In the beginning, several of our local restaurants pledged free meals to school-aged children. A handful of those restaurants are now closed. At first, I saw several upperclassmen and college students post on social media that they would offer free babysitting services for those who still had to work but had young children at home. Now those same babysitters charge by the hour when our district goes virtual to help support their own families. And for the first few months of the pandemic, teachers were essential and heroes. We went into what could only be called survival mode, and we stayed there until each student of the class of 2020 pulled up in front of the high school, climbed the steps to the front door, accepted their diploma from a gloved hand they could not shake, got back into their cars, and graduated. It was July.

Nearly a year later, uncertainty still looms in the "new normal." Some days we have A Group. Some days B Group. Some days AB Group. Some days hybrid, and some days 100 percent virtual. We wear masks, dispense hand sanitizer, clean desks before each class enters. We take temperatures before we even take roll. We call, text, email, message, snap, tweet, post, send messenger pigeons and smoke signals to our students and their parents or guardians. *Whatever it takes to reach them* we're told. But don't hug, fist bump, or high-five. *Remain six feet apart at all times*, we're told. In one day, from 8:00 a.m. to 3:15 p.m., I received ninety-eight emails from students. That does not include the interactions in person, in Google Classroom, or on Google Meet. I am exhausted. My colleagues are exhausted, and as predicted, many are on the verge of total burnout.

And so, I am reminded of that section of assigned reading from ten long months ago that I underlined: "when societies and the institutions within them change too rapidly, individuals within the institutions find it impossible to cope." I tell myself that these are *unprecedented* times, and we are in *uncharted waters*. (If you use the right COVID vernacular, things don't seem so bad.) My colleagues and I stay up into the early morning hours answering questions for nocturnal teenagers. We empathize with students turned breadwinners. We share TikToks and Tiger King memes in our group chat. We buy masks in our school colors. Yesterday, as essential county employees, teachers received the first of two shots of Moderna in the fleshy part of our biceps. Today, we self-screened for side effects and attended our first faculty meeting of 2021. We were told that 85 percent of us had gotten the first dose. Including Aaron. In twenty-eight days, we will get the second. It will be February 15, 2021.

Note: Names of people and places have been changed.

Works Cited

Hess, Abigail Johnson. "27% of Teachers Are Considering Quitting Because of Covid, Survey Finds." CNBC, December 14, 2020. www.cnbc.com/2020/12/14/27percent -of-teachers-are-considering-quitting-because-of-covid-survey.html.

LeCompte, Margaret D., and Jean J. Schensul. *Designing and Conducting Ethnographic Research: An Introduction.* 2nd edition. Walnut Creek, CA: Altamira Press, 2010.

National Education Association. "The Digital Divide and Homework Gap in Your State." October 16, 2020. www.nea.org/resource-library/digital-divide-and-homework -gap-your-state.

US Census Bureau. "QuickFacts: Russell County, Virginia." July 1, 2021. www.census .gov/quickfacts/russellcountyvirginia.

MONKEYS

The forest path is empty; and
the tourist hubbub mute. Lay's,

biscuits, banana chips, peanuts . . .
These monkeys lose the alms

from visitors. Yet they enjoy
the lockdown on the romantic

boughs without sanitizers and
masks. They foresee rain before

it kisses sand. Their infants are
beatific within cuddle and care.

They don't perforate the roof of
the earth. Genocide and lynching

are unknown to them. Never
destructive, ever serene, they

live and leave. I must mistrust
the monkey lineage of man.

JUSTICE AND RECKONING:

Colonial co-morbidities

"GEORGE FLOYD PROTESTS, COLUMBUS OHIO, MAY 2020," PHOTOGRAPH
ADAM J. GELLINGS, 2020

HOW TO MAKE WHITE SUPREMACY GENERATIVE/HOW TO SURVIVE A PANDEMIC

———

You will be made to think of yourself as hazardous. Toxic. Waste.

You will be afraid of touching others. Told you should not touch others. Touch yourself.

You will be seen as a predator. Marked as contagion. Your body, a weapon. Your intimacy, suspect.

You will be told: You do not understand viruses, how health systems work. You know nothing. Are too political. Not enough. You are ignoring other issues. Are another issue. Special one. Wait. This is not your time. You are not pivoting fast enough; you should already be creating, organizing, innovating ways to be digitally consumed online. Monetize this moment. Make it work for you, like 9/11. Make genocide generative. You are not topical. Irrelevant to the moment, you will be forgotten. Seize it.

You are too far from the source of the center, outside quarantine zones, your narrative does not matter. Even though your family is ill; your home, you were just there. You cannot stop reading, refresh; calling, donate; emailing, do whatever you can; stop this. You wonder if you shouldn't have left. Not leaving is always on your mind. As are your dead. Which you could be multiplying. You are not deserving of any test you will fail anyway. This is the language of the virus.

Wait three days before reading this. Three days after reading this, you can touch someone again, touch your face again.

Every self-loving fluid your body produces something they want to seal off. Encase in lace. Self-contained, you must be. Show no cracks in your veneers. Be polite-white-perfect. Put a doily on it. Not be a troublemaker. You do not want the police, military called. If they are called, you must kneel, enact a performance of perfect citizenship, even if you are not a citizen. Even if they are far from perfect. This is how you perfect the pandemic. This is how you make it pay. How you are made to pray, give thanks, for being here. Cross yourself.

You take notes and send it to another (anti)body. Our notes of this will be erased. Confiscated and conscripted, we must make an archive against the re-ordered records of the hate state. Dig in against the dearth of data. If our archives are housed in multiple locations, it is more difficult to erase us from the official narrative. Too many libraries to burn, files to delete. Back up, back up, keep your hands visible, re-distribute. Wipe away tear gas. Milken your pepper-sprayed eyes. Batons and rubber bullets bounce off skulls once intact. In a time of hatreds. Record this memory of us (not) touching. Our lips (un)locked. Hands (un)twined. Letters braid with mine. Enbrine.

Preserved in salt, we are ancient pathogens. Generations of pathology passed down upon us. Let us unscroll our holy helices, so many stories in so many pairs, un- and re-folding, we combine. Some new matrix of meaning, we mélange, bedrock-method this methane for later release. Local species will be replaced. We seep up through the cracks.

Bodies are stacked, one upon another, sometimes share a bag. Our liquids and gasses exceed their containers. One, two, thousands, amass a grave. Drones deliver not births, screenshot hulls of hills hollowed. Heartless islands. Conservatives circle-jerk contagion. Gussy up a genocide, genuflect in retrospect, gaslight their soundbites. Cold trucks, not filled with ice cream, toll trolls, underbridge, maskless summer, not for we. Patriotism proselytizes punches, pulled-back triggers. Such acceptable losses. Unfriendliest of fires. Inconsequential, as long as mail-sorting machines can be repurposed to sort bodies, shred ballots. We will be blamed for colonial co-morbidities, uncounted in a census ended early. Only whites worthy of enumeration. Perhaps a property requirement can be reinstated, upon this graveyard, perhaps a man speak, make decisions for his household, suffrage be revoked. Endless dreams of delusional despots. Deplorables goosestep; duck, duck, dictator. Predators flash, grenades; pundits stroke, sound cannons. A square is cleared. A book, bunkered, undone.

Shut up, the voice telling you is not your own. If you were more dead, you would feel less guilty. Only dead should hold pencils, type phantom keys.

The weight of all things not written upon your chest sits, each unspoken subject, indexed, unscribed mark, erased, makes it more difficult to breathe, finish a sentence. You do not have time to catalog an accurate inventory of assaults.

Fragment and run-on, all moments, shrapnel, enter this one. You cannot stop writing about everything else. Feel bad for not writing, when you do. Weight of the interwoven constricts your rib cage, each splintering breath excised glock-stops your glottal.

More directly, obliquely, you should not write about things at all, work trash, make a fire from it.

Child of lung-cancer loss; winter of whooping cough, bronchitis, pneumonia; caved ribs; you will be suspicious of each symptom. Scared to share you might have symptoms. Don't want to lose your job. End up homeless again. You will be scared to cough in rooms all by yourself for fear others will hear you through the walls. You become suspicious of your own body. And others. You listen as walls murmur.

As if not testing could protect you from dying, harming others. You, legion, lesion, have been here before.

Even though we are leaders of most movements, as queer/trans people of color, we are often last to be considered worthy of speaking on something.

We are footnotes to an ancillary text. Last-minute-added essay. Extra-credit critique. What would it mean if we were recognized as the first speaking on something? Perhaps we could save lives. Perhaps the lives we save could be our own.

You are not the only only one to be creating a first will and testament.

You will be counting bodies in a time of counting bodies. The U.S. never knows what to do with its bodies. With brown bodies.

This is not the first time straight white Christian men have thought their lives are worth more than others. Have the right to infect others with disease. Spit upon us, as if sidewalk. Unfold this blanket; confirm the hypothesis of our experiment. You are a controlled group. Expendable. Only once we are dead will their full freedom be exercised, excised, exorcised.

The choosing of bodies to live begins before the choice of where the ventilators and masks and gloves and bleach wipes go and don't go. It's where these hospitals were on the land centuries prior, who was allowed to enter them, who never returned, who still die on land that is and is not ours.

We are choosing bodies to live.

We breathe in the ashes of our dead. One day, we will tell you the rest of the cremaining story.

This was once a grave. Bodies were buried here. Before this became a graveyard, children danced, lovers necked, elders walked with care. This land has seen so many alterations, fill-ins and drainages of swamp. Underground rivers still flow; salt still washes up on shore. Our dead keep on gathering above and below the soil.

Digital copies will be disseminated to avoid cross-contamination. There are different strains. There is a strain in speaking about this.

I will tape this smiling picture on my chest; you know you can be safe with me.

Let me adjust your mask.

Previously published in *Mizna*

BLACKOUT

———

Black man, black shirt,
Black hoodie, black pants,

Black mother, black son,
Gone.

Black man, black shirt,
Black hoodie, black pants,

Black widow,

Black man, black shirt,
Black hoodie, black pants,

Black man, black shirt,
Black hoodie, black pants,

Black son, with no father

Black man, black shirt,
Black hoodie, black pants,

Black shadow

Black man, black shirt,
Black hoodie, black pants,

Black box

Black man, black shirt,
Black hoodie, black pants,

Black hearse

Black man, black shirt,
Black hoodie, black pants,

Black man, black box,

Black hearse

Black man, black shirt,
Black hoodie, black pants,

Blackhole, black man

Poetry | *Kim Denning*

THE MARROW-SUCKING GRIP
OF IMMIGRATION INJUSTICE

———————

About those ones, those thoughts,
        the ones that keep you
                spineless.

They roll around inside your bones.

        Eating the marrow.

    Sucking it down.
        Sliding away.
             Until you don't know
             it's gone.

I've got a hold, you think, a pin in the axle.
Keeping things turning.
One step after another.

        But the grip of   security   has   sweaty palms.

    It slips,   sliding sideways, frontways,
        backways,

              everyone else's way
              but yours.

It's their bullshit,   you know,
their fears you carry,
                staring back in your mirrors,
        the one predictable,
the rearview that haunts.

                And there isn't fuck all that you can do.

Poetry | *Roan Davis*

WHITE

———

An absence of color that, coincidently, makes its own color.
A fairly new concept; "What is it to be white?"
I've been scrutinized and played down by such spiteful white
  eyes.
I, however, have been mixed with too much of one or the other on
  the great artist's palette. A child of two worlds.
Too white to be Korean and too yellow to be white.
I have no place to call my own.
I was told to go back to the Land of Dragons.
Insulted in one breath while "my people" are praised for their
  food in another.
All in the same hour.
If I was more open and honest with that lady, so happily munch-
  ing on her egg roll, what could I have said?
What will they do if they discover
the gods they so revere come from Asia?
That the fairies they mention
Hail from the lands of naan
That the originals were replaced with the fae
As they know them.
It's not Europe where the pride comes from
But a sick perversion of the white american dream
What would Odin say to these naysayers that would gaze
Upon his almond all-knowing eye?
The hate being spat, what if it indicates
A need for something to call their own
After being grafted into lands, not entirely their original home?

The sins of the ancestors are a hefty burden, I should know.
I feel half of that guilt even still as a person of color.
Yet an example of the color white should be followed.
It is still able to make its own
In the absence of all this color.

Poetry | *Liseli A. Fitzpatrick*

WE'VE BEEN HERE BEFORE

————————

we've been here
before bound
face to face
with the unknown
shoved into tight
spaces, shackled,
strangled by the
suffocating,
unsanitized
stench of capitalism and
communicable diseases
unable to breathe
muzzled behind iron masks
savagely uprooted and   s c a t t e r e d
across   sugar plantations   and   white   cotton fields

forced to reimagine home
in slums and shanties
with no running water or
happy birthday songs
to wash our hands
or toilet paper
or food
because
we could not
eat what we

reaped
gathered bones
black and brown
bodies thrown into
unmarked graves

    we were here before
    carried in the resilient
    blood of our ancestors
    who with girded loins
    transported us across
    their backs dismantling
    systems with their own tools
    quilting fabrics from scraps
    Soul-stirring delicacies like songs
divining
altars and organs
in their lungs
    because,
    the earth is a tabernacle
    and the body   an instrument
    and the heart   a beat
    and God only comes alive
    when we dance

we've been here
before
standing on
the shoulders
of the ancestors
who taught us
    how to make
something

out of nothing
and summon
light out of darkness
fear not, we've been here before

Previously published in *About Place Journal* and *A (Re)Turn to the African Girl: (Re)Defining African Girlhood Studies* edited collection

"PROTEST," DIGITAL COLLAGE · JODY ZELLEN, 2020

Poetry | *Ahimsa Timoteo Bodhrán*

CROSSTOWN

—————

i.
snakes turn the pages, hold your place,
till you re-turn, with gloves;
each marble step depressed
by footfalls of those before me

ii.
before diaspora, the people of the third book practice,
perfect amnesia; generations after reconcile
records of all the soulless; those that survive, not
turned to salt, acquiesce to archives of the latest saints

iii.
before bankruptcy, black robes are laundered;
never fully clean, non-idle hands arrest the night,
extinguish all light: candles, small children's
wings—clipped, cloistered, collateral

iv.
crowned, colonial cartographers confiscate, conceive cages;
canaric, comorbid, choirs concord the canon, concoct chimera;
cardinals contest contagion, charlatan charismata counter
        complicity;
crosstown, corona counts coup, collects coffins, coughs up blood

—————

This poem previously appeared in *PRISM international*

MY UNCERTAIN STORY

———

I could hear my mother from my bedroom preparing her lunch in the kitchen: a beef and bean burrito, a yogurt cup, some almonds and diced mandarins. She's healthy and loves her greens. My mother has always been a hard worker but recently because of my weekly court dates, daily community service hours, and outpatient counseling, she started working a lot more.

I had just completed my usual routine of community service hours and working with my dad, so I was taking a nap. I could hear my mom's footsteps creaking down the stairs to the garage. I thought, *she must not want to wake me up.* This would be the last time I was going to see her for a very long time. I tried to get up but my body felt like a dead limb. I tried to talk, but no words came out. It was as if my mind and body were completely disconnected. My heart started beating faster and faster as I lay there in distress. I was sleep paralyzed. This occasionally happened when my body was depleted of all its energy. "She can't leave, I have to say goodbye." "A . . . Ama!" I said out loud in fright as I woke up from my nightmare.

"Hijo, what's wrong? Why are you screaming?" she said as she entered through my bedroom door.

"I heard you leaving. . . . I—I thought you were gonna leave without saying goodbye." She sat at the edge of the bed next to me and extended her arm.

"Come here. I wouldn't just leave. I'm still here, son." I hugged her and placed my head on her chest. I closed my eyes to prevent the tears from falling, but they found their way out. Lying on my mother I could feel her pain; she yearned to go with me, as if the sheer force of her will could rectify my circumstances.

That evening my mother went to work, and my father drove me to court. We parked and stood outside his F-150. As he gazed into the door of the court, he said, "Uh, I think I'll stay in the truck." I didn't blame him. I knew it would hurt him more than it would hurt me.

"It's okay, Dad. I didn't want you to come in." I had been in drug court for over a year and it was finally ending. Only this ending was the beginning of a very uncertain journey. I walked up the courthouse stairs knowing I would come out in chains. I have always been a kind, respectful man, who wears his heart on his sleeve. Maybe I haven't been your model citizen, but I sure as hell am not a criminal.

"Mr. Hernandez, I hereby sentence you to the maximum of one county year for your DUI." No one saw this coming, I had completed outpatient, I was going to all my meetings and completing all my community service hours, but I had a slip-up. I came up positive for alcohol on one of my drug tests. Recovery is no casual walk in the park; it takes dedication, time, and honesty. Relapse is part of it, but when you're in a program like drug court, relapse isn't forgiven.

I remember the deep embarrassment I felt at being cuffed in front of all my friends and counselors I had known for the past year. Cynical failure looped my mind. I was an adult male with no job, no car, living off my parents in the basement. I felt hopeless and without a purpose. I needed to better myself emotionally and spiritually. I needed to work on what dedications maneuvered my actions. Maybe some time away to reground was exactly what I needed, but why did it have to be jail?

The court officer walked me from the podium, to some secluded chairs on the side. Moments later everyone started walking out. I sat there uncomfortable with my hands cuffed behind my back. A cold and despairing feeling passed through my body, I felt completely alone. The next court crowd punctually walked in, and the officers waited until everyone sat down for them to casually walk me out. I guess my punishment starts now. I tried to keep my head up as I walked out the courtroom, but humility laid heavy on me. Some people looked at me with confusion, maybe wondering about my story. Some ignored my presence, but most stared.

November 13, 2019, was the first time I had ever set foot in jail. As they processed me, they placed me in a holding cell where the floors were painted dark green, which reminded me of my high school gym. The walls were a dull beige like an old hospital. What kind of combination was that? As a professional painter, seeing patterns like these made me cringe. They brought me to a walk-in shower where they stripped me and my dignity. I felt degraded and mortified to be told to turn around and squat. "Now, cough." This wasn't the only time they practiced this method, every time they gave you a random cell inspection, they made you strip. Every time you went for a visit, they made you strip.

I was given a hideous, oversized orange jumpsuit to wear, with the words INMATE printed on the right leg and RCJ on the back. Just in case you ever forgot who you were and where you were staying. Two sheets, two blankets. A roll of toilet paper that felt more like sandpaper and of course instantly dissolved once it got in contact with water. A tiny toothbrush with a tiny toothpaste. I was then told to walk and find my wing and my cell, number 8. Which was also my new nickname, Number Eight. People don't care enough to ask you for your name.

I found my cell and inside I saw one bed, one toilet, and one sink. Phew. One less thing I have to worry about. I am a gay man, so thinking of sleeping with a roommate in jail is a little nerve wracking. You never know who you're gonna pair up with.

I was astounded at the sight of everyone in this twilight zone, where the same group of people sat around and did the same routine every day. They looked like bodies without souls. One man stood out from the crowd, he sat right in front of the TV. He wore sadness like a fur coat, it weighed heavy on his shoulders. He aimlessly stared into the TV, like he was staring into the abyss. Other people played cards or walked outside, whatever they did they did it every day at the same exact time. This was going to be my new life, and slowly but surely, I became one of these despairing people.

Time was vanishing into oblivion and it was also going so slow. In the outside world, you would be able to distinguish "Taco Tuesday" from "Hump day" or "Friday night" from "Sunday brunch," but not here; weekdays and weekends meant nothing. Thanksgiving came around, which was nice because we were all given an extra nugget for dinner.

Our dinner was seven nuggets, instead of six, a boiled potato and some overcooked peas.

Then Christmas came, New Year's, and then my mother's birthday, which was actually really hard on me. I lay in my cell and reminisced about those wonderful days. I used to always make sure there were lots of flowers placed all over the house, and then for dinner I would take her out to a nice restaurant. My mother was able to visit me, which was great. I was able to give her a kiss and a hug, only instead of making me feel any better I felt worse as I watched her leave. Now that I think about it, that's how I felt every time she would visit. Sometimes I couldn't even enjoy the forty-five-minute visits because I was already upset that she would leave.

A month after my mother's birthday coronavirus hit, and it hit hard. The whole world shut down. I remember listening to the radio and news, trying to get any information about the pandemic. It was surreal. The correctional officers (COs) would say how lucky we were, that we were the safest people around. We didn't feel like that. There's nothing worse than feeling hopeless toward the ones you love and care for the most. My mother, who is in her late fifties and works as a janitor, is high-risk and could easily catch it. My brother works in the city and is even more exposed. What if he got infected and brought it back to his wife and kids?

Living in a confined environment changes you, it either makes you or breaks you, and only the people who have lived through it can understand. Most days it's you and your crazy thoughts and all you do is think about the negative things that can and will happen.

Around June was when this surreal pandemic became real to us. The facility started implementing a bunch of new rules, everyone started wearing masks and enforcing social distancing. We started to get concerned and wondered when we would get masks, but they never gave us any. For mealtime, usually four people would sit at a table, now only two could sit together. This made no sense because the rest of the time we would be crowded up next to each other. They took away our basketballs, handballs and board games. Although that may not seem like such a big deal, these items were essential to us. This is what we used during our leisure time. They also stopped visiting, which also stopped AA, NA, and Bible study.

I felt like time was being wasted, so I took a trustee position to feel like I wasn't completely wasting my life away. We were four trustees, and our pay was a dollar a day; extra recreation time and any extra food was ours. My job was to mop the floors, wipe down all the tables, telephones and door handles, clean the showers, and place the garbage outside the pod. Needless to say, I didn't take the job for the great benefits or pay. At first, it was merely because you got locked in less, but as time passed on I started to become fond of the peculiar ambiance I was in while I mopped. I can't fully express why, but it was such a therapeutic exercise. Swaying left and right, back and forth, watching as the dry dull floor turned into a wet shiny room, leaving no place untouched. As I finished the room it left a sense of accomplishment and a newly refreshed fragranced room. I pictured my life as the floor, dirty and stained, and the mop as magical and could get rid of all my defects with just a simple swing.

Most days were pretty boring, although one time I almost got into a fight, which was pretty exhilarating. I just finished giving out breakfast, two cereal cups and one milk. There was extra cereal left so the trustees and I divided them equally among ourselves. One guy came up to us for more cereal. "Let me get your cereal," he said. This actually means, "Yo, give me your cereal." You can't let someone talk to you like that in jail, everyone observes how you react to things, to see if you're weak or not.

"No!" I said and grabbed my cereal and started walking away.

"Yo, give me your fucking cereal bitch or I'ma fuck you up."

"I'm not giving you my fucking cereal, go ask someone else," I said. The tension rose after I sat down on my table. I kept looking back at him and he kept looking back at me. He started talking to some guys around him. He pointed at me. They looked at me, and I looked at them. I felt so much adrenaline. I've never been in a fight, though I got beat up once when I was in elementary school. I've never been dumb enough to win an argument by physical force. I would never fight someone unless my life depended on it. It's a weird trance to be in, when you realize that you might just have a fight, right here, right now. I lost all fear, my body tensed up, my blood ran hot.

Fights started occurring daily after the pandemic, which was no surprise. They took away everything fun we could do; they left us no choice but to cause trouble. The guys would "play the cell," which was when two guys sneak into someone else's cell and fight until both decided to stop.

Once, as two guys were fighting in the open, fifteen COs charged in within seconds. They made everyone lock in. The COs tried to stop the fight, but the guys wouldn't separate. The guys got maced and everyone else paid the price. The mace quickly spread through the vents like wildfire, everyone started coughing. I quickly grabbed my towel, wet it, and clogged the vent. I placed one of my jumpers underneath the door crack and went under the covers. In jail you have to learn to adapt quickly without asking anyone for help. You never feel safe.

Eight weeks before my release the sergeant told me he was hiring me as a building trustee. I was in shock. Not just anyone gets this position. You have to be sentenced, your crime has to be nonviolent, and you can't have any warrants or holds from any states. A building trustee also gets the privilege of leaving jail eight hours before his release date. This meant that when your sentence day arrives, you can leave at midnight.

I am not a US citizen, and on my release day ICE was going to pick me up. If I had this position, I would be able to leave and not get caught by ICE. I remember perfectly when the ICE officer spoke to me, it was exactly two weeks after I arrived at jail. He asked me a bunch of questions and asked me to sign some papers, but I didn't feel comfortable so I told him I wouldn't sign anything. "You will finish your time here, Mr. Hernandez, and once you finish your time you will deal with us," he said.

After they hired me as a building trustee, I was moved to A-wing with all the other trustees, a total of four. My first shift went great. I got up at 4:30 a.m. to get ready, we started at 5:30 a.m. Of course, I had way too much time to get ready since all I had to do was put my jumper on and brush my teeth, but I was excited. I couldn't believe I was there. My pay was still a dollar a day. We also had one special job no other inmate had, which was to go outside the jail, and throw away the trash.

Outside, you could see the grass and the cars driving by from afar, and even though it was still enclosed by a gate, I swear it smelled better than the air inside our usual courtyard.

Lunch shift came by and I was in the middle of eating when one of the sergeants came over and told me to follow him. I knew this wasn't good. He then proceeded to fire me because of my ICE hold. "But the sergeant that previously hired me said that there was a way around that type of hold. I thought everything was fine when you guys moved me," I said.

"Well, I don't know what he told you, but you cannot be a building trustee." I went back to my cell, and although I had only done half a shift, I felt drained and decided to sleep. There are so many types of mind games that people play in jail, but the games the officers play are the worst. I don't think the officers know how powerful their words actually are. These symbols and vibrations manifest into physical actions that either make you or break you. Later that day the sergeant who hired me came by and explained that although he had approved the move, it wasn't up to him. It was up to the captain and they would "eventually work on it."

"Eventually." His words echoed in my mind. Eleven days went by and no news. After fourteen days one of the building trustees finished his time and left, which then only left three, and that wasn't enough. The captain was given no other choice than to request the administration to allow a man, with an ICE hold, for the first time ever, to be a building trustee. No one else was eligible. Since the pandemic started, courts had frozen; no one was getting sentenced, and the people who remained were either not sentenced or had a violent crime. A new rule had to be created because of this peculiar situation. I was hired again, only this time no one could fire me.

There were two new rules. I had to wear a different jumper of the color blue, to separate me from the rest and to show there was something different about me, and I had to be watched. Also, I couldn't take out the garbage with the rest of the trustees as that would "provide an opportunity for an escape." I started caring less and less.

They called me Baby Blue. I worked hard for my dollar, but I ate well.

Although life was plateauing, I had an ominous feeling harassing my shoulders daily. I sporadically thought of my life in the United States. How great I have had it, and how great it could continue to be. I also thought about what life back in Mexico would be like if I got deported.

Where would I live? Would everyone in my family accept me with open arms? What are they even like? I don't have a college degree— would I be able to get a job easily without one? I thought of my parents. *I can't get deported. But there's nothing I can do.* My thoughts were constantly at war. These habitual negative thoughts were unwillingly becoming my daily prayers. What would happen to all my belongings? The people and loved ones I had made relationships with, would they just disappear? Why must I suffer for something that wasn't in my control? I was brought here when I was nine. I didn't choose to come here. I didn't choose to make this country my home, and the United States is all I've ever known. I felt like I was getting deported from my own country.

My release date was July 3, 2020—one county year meant eight months with good time. My birthday was July 6. How perfect was that? I was getting out right on time. I thought of planning a small get-together with my family and loved ones who had kept in contact with me.

Which, by the way, weren't many. People contact you, write letters, even come and visit for the first two weeks, but after that they forget about you. Your calls don't get answered anymore, and the letters stop getting mailed. I thought of working around the house with my dad, and maybe even going back to school. I was beginning to get motivated for life outside jail, and it was nice for a change to feel good inside, while being in such a horrible place.

A few weeks went by and most Cos knew I had an ICE hold. The topic was inevitable. Some would joke about how I should make a run for it as soon as I got out the front door. They would tell me of their favorite resort spots they loved in Mexico, and that I should get a job there, to hook them up with a free room. They said that I should hit up my uncle, El Chapo, to help me out with one of his tunnels. Some would try to comfort me and tell me that I was getting out a day before the Fourth of July and that ICE wouldn't show up. Some inmates would also join in the conversations and would tell me that it wasn't that bad getting deported. That coming back wasn't that hard. Some of them had done it multiple times, and that for Mexicans, it was much cheaper. No one cared to ask what I wanted to do if I got deported, and I never mentioned to anyone that I wanted to come back, they just assumed. It's kind of funny now, thinking back, how my life's problems seem to only be a speck on the road for everyone else, and how everyone seems to think that they know the answers to my life's problems. I felt like a soldier waiting dormant for the war.

I submitted my request to be released at midnight before my release date, and I was approved! That night I gave away all my books, commissary, cosmetics, and clothing just like anyone else that leaves, and said my goodbyes. I called my mom to tell her the good news. She told me that three of my friends called and asked if I had gotten the approval. They wanted to be outside when I got out. My family and friends all gathered outside the jail at 11:30 p.m. I stayed up listening to music.

It was finally 11:30 p.m. Then midnight. Then 12:30, then 12:45, but my door never opened. As every dragging minute passed by, any little noise I heard from a closing or opening door made my heart skip a beat. I thought, "This is the CO that will pop my door. Surely someone has made a mistake somewhere and realized it late." But nothing. Lying on my bed staring at the four hideous green brick walls, I felt my adrenaline mix with anger. There was a knot in my throat, like I was choking on pain. "How could they do this to me? I was approved and I was on the schedule to be released!" I felt devalued, demoralized. I felt taken advantage of. I've always been a passive man, expecting justice when justice is needed, but life isn't always fair and sometimes it sucks.

I thought about my family gathered outside, and how they had wasted their time by coming here, just to be told to leave because no one by the name of Hernandez was getting out. I couldn't help but feel at fault, and I took blame for this. I think that although I had paid my debt by serving time, I hadn't fully forgiven myself for the pain I had cost my loved ones, especially my mom. I could see the worry, sadness, and hurt in her eyes every time she came to see me.

Eventually, 5:30 a.m. came and all the trustees woke up and were released from their cell for work. I didn't sleep and no one dared say a word to me. Once they saw me, they figured out what had happened. On the way to the kitchen we passed the lieutenant's office. I could have gone in and asked why I wasn't released, but knowing why wouldn't have made a difference.

I started my routine, like usual, only this time I had a new trustee, Tony, shadowing me. Tony and I had become good friends, which is not very common in jail. I asked Tony if he could do intake on his own. I felt odd, and for some reason I didn't want to go to intake at all. I guess my intuition was looking out for me. When Tony came back he said, "Noe, I wasn't going to tell you this, but I think I should either way. ICE is here, they picked up your file and they're ready for you." I felt my heart sink, like a cement brick, into the pit of my stomach. I felt a cold sweat on my forehead. At this very moment I knew exactly what was going to happen. I finished my shift early, because who the hell cares about cleaning dishes when they're about to be picked up by ICE?

After grabbing my few belongings, they called me down to intake, but there was no one from immigrations there. "So, I'm good to go after here?" I asked the officer.

"Yeah, you just have to change and sign a release form and you're a free man!" he said very enthusiastically.

"Free man? Umm . . . is anyone here for me?"

"Huh, what do you mean? Like your ride? I'm not sure what you're asking me." He lied straight to my face, telling me that there were no problems.

I took off the oversized blue jumpsuit and put my old clothes back on. A pink fitted undershirt , a gunmetal button-down Armani Exchange shirt, tight khaki pants and Nikes. They all felt so comfortable. The officer walked me down the famous long cold hallway that everyone always stares at when they pass by it, the exit. I firmly held my clear huge garbage bag, filled with my personal belongings. I was prepared. And ready to embrace what was about to occur.

As soon as the door opened, five men surrounded me. I didn't notice them; their voices became distorted and they faded into the distance as my mind slipped away. It was a typical New York morning in July, the humidity felt like a heavy blanket. I could smell the rich green grass freshly cut, the sky was gray and melancholy. It was about to rain, how very cliché. My vision tunneled as soon as I saw my mom, she was standing next to the flagpole by the roundabout with my best friend, Tannia. It had been over six months since I had last seen her, and all I wanted to do was hold her in my arms, feel her warm motherly love, and tell her that everything was going to be okay. While all of this was happening, the ICE officer started cuffing my arms and legs, an old too-familiar feeling. "We're going to let you say goodbye to your mom and friend," he said. He walked me to them, my mother's tears poured down her eyes, and the mask she wore absorbed them like a sponge. It was a pretty mask, it had a watermelon print. I couldn't actually hug her, but I managed to place my neck tightly on her right shoulder. I did the same with Tannia. I felt nothing, I was numb, I was too busy taking it all in.

After what seemed to be a few seconds they walked me to their gray van with blacked-out tints and we started to ride off, the destination was the ICE detention center, an hour upstate in Goshen. We circled around the flagpole where mom and Tannia still stood. Tannia held my mom as mom poured her eyes out. All she could do was watch helplessly as her child was taken away from her again, but this time with no reassurance that he would get out. I close my eyes and I can relive the nightmare again and again. I will never forget this moment when ICE detained me. And sadly unlike this sentence, my uncertain story does not end here.

Poetry | *Deidra Suwanee Dees*

EM ONTVLECETV / INVADED

———

you invaded my space with anti-climactic explosion,
you purged my tongue with a new breed of speech,

Vhopvketv Muscogee values descend upon erosion,
how can you still drive me into retreat?
Your support for Jews in the Holocaust
makes me want to believe you hold empathy,
Opunvkv my Indigenous voice is almost lost,
why can't I convince you to believe in me?
when Muscogees ruled, we had enough to eat,
children went to sleep at night in a safe place,
Enokketv there were no murderous police or COVID disease,

but now you behold an emaciated race;
vanished sacred land that belonged to me,
I am the essence of a dying turtle's call,
Asomkita you've stolen everything—even my dignity,

how can you hurt me more when i've already lost it all?

———

This poem previously appeared in *Little Blue Marble*

Poetry | *Jameka Hartley*

POV[1]

———

Black mothers have been tired
Long before COVID
That is shameful
Rest is revolution
Black women are magic but
I'll tell you this
We're human
Superwoman is fiction
Take that nap
Weep
Wail
Black woman, you are inherently worthy
Let me say
It's all incredibly hard
Days bleeding into night
Zoom, zoom, zoom
Home/Life/Work/Life/Life/Life
Blurred lines
But it won't always be this way
People are selfish and stubborn
I've observed that
Not living by the Golden Rule
Yet

———

1   This is a reverse poem that can be read backward or forward.

I believe we are better than this
One day
Our dead will be honored properly
"Save Us!", cries the world to Black Women
Black Women Save Black Women
Black Women mother Black Women
And all may benefit
Black mothers are divinity defined

"GEORGE FLOYD PROTESTS, COLUMBUS OHIO, JUNE 2020,"
PHOTOGRAPH · ADAM J. GELLINGS, 2020

THE HOME OF THE BRAVE

———

Police blow
up the television set,
forcing open the door
of no return. Slides
racked, rounds live,
with nightsticks
and body parts
arming their weight,
they press,

unloading freedom
on America

to drive desire
beyond the threshold
through heaven. Civil
but ballistic, we've asked
peacefully to listen to
the pleas for breath, yet
still they've kept pressing.

It's a thick, diesel
atmosphere out here.
Authorities push leverage
until god is found
inside somebody's skull

and tear gas and obscenities
in our airways, as we gasp
for clean air. Sirens echo
howls of communities.

Not everyone gets the TV
and the morphine when
the hate crimes hit the bone
so we go to the streets
in search of what we can't
load on our screens.

Chloe x Halle sing
the Star-Spangled Banner
before kickoff. The sound
is sweet, but my hand gets heavy
placing it over my heart swelling.

THINGS I NEVER TOLD YOU

———

I've been mugged twice. Both incidents involved
white men who were much older than me at the time.
I didn't realize I had so much in common with the rest of the
    world.
I've been punched without warning
after being mistaken for somebody else more than once,
which would seem high on the scale of random aggression
until you take into account the Indigenous in me.
I would say more but large swaths of the heartland haven't for-
    given me for existing.
Once, I climbed onto my best friend's roof because
he asked if I could. It was the same weekend we spent
more time as pirates than boys, and I discovered a talent for
    sacrifice.
I let hundreds, probably thousands die in the pursuit
of imaginary doubloons, and though it was just a game,
it signaled a pattern which would follow me long
after we left the ocean in our wake.
Twice, my body has attempted to snuff out its own pilot.
When I hear words like septic or necrotic, I usually think
of sanitation or Halloween. I don't picture an autonomic nervous
system reaching for the breakers and trying to turn out the lights.
I didn't imagine how cold a body becomes when its fire goes out.
I didn't plan to turn the car heater on in the middle of summer
in Yucaipa, which is about ten degrees cooler than the lowest pit
    of Hell,
and smells about the same. I didn't sketch out plans in my head

about ways to burn my skin in the shower to restart my core.
I didn't think about health insurance or life insurance,
or what it means to grind your bones sixty hours a week
for the promise of a stranger holding a net when you fall.
Now it's all I think about as I wash my hands.

ENVIRONMENT AND PLACE:

Let the river turn the stone

"CATSKILLS 1," PHOTOGRAPH · JUDEA COSTES, 2021

Poetry | *Lisa Suhair Majaj*

LINES BEFORE LOCKDOWN

———

The yellow daisies down the street are not yet
on lockdown. They sprawl across the sidewalk

in proud profusion, a luminous bastion guarding
the empty lot. *Chrysanthemum coronarium*

they are called: beacons of regal joy. They brighten
a world awash with the virus bearing their name,

the illness now cresting tsunami-like toward us—
we human oases, on islands of many kinds,

clustered within borders about to close.
We are about to learn about life and death

and limits and courage and care; to learn that bastions
offer less defense than humanity, and that we

are not unique. (In Gaza, where the lockdown
that for us spells life threatens yet more death,

instead of panic there is weary knowledge.
Gazans are willing to teach the world how to survive

a closure without end, without exit, without hope.)
Here in Cyprus the spring sun shines erratically,

climate change altering the steadiness of our days.
I search for the sun's corona, that gaseous halo

veiling its orb—but it is only visible during total eclipse,
and we have not yet reached the eclipse.

The virus floats invisibly among us: medieval maces
studded with threat. Sparrows twitter in the olive tree,

silvery overgrowth hiding the twist of trunk. The narcissus
I planted last year shyly raises its stamened corona

as swallows wheel above, oblivious to restrictions.
The sky is calm, the moon's shroud not yet visible

in late day's sky. I think of the sea, forbidden to us now—
that blue expanse, its currents salted and surging,

tumbling with bitter knowledge, with sea-smoothed stone—
then fill my lungs with breath and plunge to lockdown.

"CLEMATIS," INTAGLIO PRINT · GLORIA GOGUEN, 2020

HYMN

───────

After that time we sang but never spoke
of the fatigue and confusion when
crows ran crazy in the sky
as we rushed toward the brittle field
past the world's debris
the mounds of bones and hats.

Was there time left to mow and
let the river turn the stone
and the ovens reshape the grain?
Who in this nightmare has the power
to quell the sun from burning up the wheat
or command the moon to wash her face and hands?

The only unbroken circle was the stone
sleeping beside the cold oven.
The shrieking crows masked our song
and the stain on her crescent face remains.

"VILLAGE," OIL AND GOUACHE ON 100% RAG PAPER
CAROLINE FURR, 2020

Poetry | *Lukpata Lomba Joseph*

MAY SHIVERS

———

Morning currents lured
down the spine
of a palm frond, and leaves
fondled a rust-kissed roof. I
saw—through blemished glasses
of my window—
two sparrows
ricocheting from tall
to medium baobabs without
an ounce
of pandemic conscience.
In the minutes that followed,
I would dare the gods
with wild violets from an old lady.

Poetry | *Alan Smith Soto*

FOR THE EMPTIERS HAVE EMPTIED THEM OUT

———

(Nahum 2:2)
I looked out the window
at the evicted street.
It happened to be raining.
It happened to be April, 2020.
No gasoline rainbow skidded
to the gutter,
like a discarded dream,
no need for time
to push the tower's gears to
the edge,
or sirens to run
behind themselves.
Everything removed its emptiness.
Why the window pane
did not shatter
is beyond me.

Poetry | *Aimee Nicole*

WHILE THE WORLD FELL APART AROUND US

———————

We forged space for something new.
We met in empty Market Basket parking lots
and fogged up the windows of my Santa Fe.
We treated golf courses like our own private islands.
Dreams, the string we puppeteered under starry nights
with no one to tell us no.
Borders melted away by the fearless fist of dreaming.

"CATSKILLS 5," PHOTOGRAPH · JUDEA COSTES, 2021

"CATSKILLS 9," PHOTOGRAPH · JUDEA COSTES, 2021

A COVID SPRING COMES TO SOUTHEAST PENNSYLVANIA

This morning I put two jars and a DVD
in a plastic bag, drive over
to my friend's house, leave it by her door.
This feels like a vacation, an escape
from the house, fifteen minutes
to hear songs on a homemade CD.

Then back home, the crabapple in bloom,
irises thickening purple stalks.
I talk to them now,
not keeping six feet away. Spring,
precious, ephemeral,
like the redbud,
done blooming just yesterday.

I try to keep spring from leaving,
call out to it. From the porch,
I watch it go.

Previously published in *Viral Imaginations*

2020

Turns out high time for all to stand still, as
I stay at home every day, trying to find
How to hold my stream of consciousness

& a ship floats around beyond the harbor
Anchoring itself among sharks and whales
Swimming against dark-blue undercurrents

There is also a fully loaded truck parked
By the roadside, like an old thought lost
In a heavy traffic held up long at twilight

& airplanes perching amid the trees. There is
An unmasked woman in the adjacent house
Sitting motionlessly, as if pondering whether

To reset her clock, like a lonely traveler
Hesitating which road to take, or God Him-
Self pausing to reset Earth on a new orbit

FOLDED UP

---

like Swiss army knives,
the amusement rides lay low
in a vacant lot
between the Division of Highways
and a used car dealership
along West Virginia Route 33,
the Ferris un-wheeled,
the bumper cars going nowhere
in standstill traffic,
the Scrambler's arms surrendering,
the Tilt-A-Whoa,
the wooden horses of the carousel
lame as lucky rabbits' feet
taking shelter
in boarded-up carnival games,
all silent as baseballs
that no one throws,
even carnies frightened to breathe
the air once filled with sawdust,
cotton candy, corn dogs and vomit,
now a symptom, like the fever
of running down the midway,
the tiredness,
the shortness of breath
after the Roulette,
a gamble no one is willing to take.

Poetry | *Fred Shaw*

SOCIAL DISTANCE

———

Even before this began, I found myself
watching the neighbors getting tossed
out of that rental with peeling brown paint,
their husky and chihuahua no longer
standing guard, barking at crunchy leaves
and joggers blowing by. Just days before,
on an afternoon walk, I'd waved from across
the two-lane we both called home,
speeding cars keeping us at arm's-length
while the husband and wife smoked,
their little boy's headless action figures
strewn about the porch, one resting
against a three-legged kitchen chair.
Now, with their rusty Ford Ranger gone,
a dingy stars-and-stripes sways there
just above a patch of mud
as the difficult talent of a white Frigidaire
cools in that tiny yard, emptied of its ketchup
and canned beer, the bottom door swinging
slowly in the traffic's steady wash.

———

Previously published in *American Journal of Poetry*

AUSTIN

———

It is odd watching the city shut down,
one venue at a time. SxSW, gone.
Our church went virtual a week ago.
Days before, the choir director had called,
"We will not meet or sing this Sunday,"
an odd phrasing. The monthly poetry meeting
was canceled after the feature backed out.
Our acting president has been working
seven days a week to keep the nursing homes
clean, if not safe. The writing group
is moving online. My extroverted wife
looks forward to it. This surprises me.

I can imagine a white pastor preaching
to a video camera in an empty sanctuary.
But Black pastors? Struggling to preach call
with no response. Can there be worship
without congregation, musicians, and choir?

The university and the schools
shut down yesterday as the first
COVID-19 cases in Austin
were announced. Full baskets of
toilet paper, ramen, paper towels,
bottled water, and pasta queued up
with six packs of liter Cokes

straddling the rails. We are using
old rags as paper towels.

Like hearing a train start.
The slam slam slam
of each car starting up
is coming closer.

I know how the train starting up ends.
How does this end?

Previously published in *Tejascovido* and *Langdon Review of the Arts*

"MOTHER'S DAY," ALCOHOL INK · CHRISTINE L. VILLA, 2020

HOPE: *Beyond sorrow there's a gardenia tree*

"HAWTHORNE," DIGITAL PAINTING
EDWARD MICHAEL SUPRANOWICZ, 2020

DURING QUARANTINE, I EMBRACE MYSELF AS A LONG-HAULER,

———

lignum vitae, wood
so dense it doesn't float

I've been reduced to not being able to stand up in the shower

poetic, considering how much
the wood has given to ocean travel

Even reading a book is challenging and exhausting

an escaped ornamental
pruned to maintain a narrower profile

I don't understand what's happening in my body

the leaf is made of more
than one leaf-like part

Every day you wake up and you might have a different symptom

from a distance
like clouds of purple

I've had messages saying this is all in your head

as the non-native is not invasive
at the northernmost range

I understand there are so many unknowns

not so easily warped by humidity
or temperature changes

As a patient, I need acknowledgment

as a generalization, then,
it suffers from a reputation as slow

It has gotten better, but I track that trajectory in weeks, not days

similar to pomegranate seeds
either one is a worthwhile endeavor

Being a survivor is something you must also survive

Previously published in *About Place Journal*

MAGDALENA

———

Beyond sorrow
there's a gardenia tree
that bursts open
with a fragrance so sweet
you cannot doubt her
soft devotion.

And with each hour,
she thoughtlessly drops petals
like a rosary spilling white
prayer beads onto city corners
reminding:
      stay gentle
stay tender.

Beyond sorrow, you find yourself
opening until all your colors
delicately
generously
      desperately
spill over onto quiet sidewalks
with a fragrance so sweet
the gardenia herself cannot doubt
your wild devotion.

And, in discovering your
sweetness, leans close
and gifts you her blooming flowers.
You'll think, I can be in no better place.

TOO LOUD TO SLEEP

———

I perform in front of my iMac, repeating the same words over and over so my ninth grade English Language Development students can practice hearing and speaking academic vocabulary. The class's intention is to prepare students for reclassification from English Language Learner to English Proficient. I tell the students to turn their microphones off. Otherwise, a cacophonous symphony of asynchronous voices and internet lag would reverberate through all our computers. During the pandemic, at least this is one thing we can be saved from.

I watch my students' mouths move on screen. I don't know if they are emitting sound.

Distance teaching requires trust.

I ask students to brainstorm guesses into chat: *How many hours of sleep do adolescents need?*

Most answer nine.

I ask: *What time do you usually go to bed?*

Most say ten.

Since school begins at 9 a.m., I wonder why they are still tired: *Are they falling asleep at night?*

I ask straight from the workbook: *What are some reasons adolescents fail to get sufficient sleep?* I explain to my students that sufficient means adequate or enough.

The Zoom chat fills: loud neighbors, loud parties, loud music, loud cars racing down the street.

My students live in a section of Los Angeles with one of the highest rates of Covid.

They don't say Covid keeps them awake at night.

I wonder what else keeps them awake: *la migra, desempleo, hambre,* Trump.

What realities are they afraid to speak? Thoughts are immaterial until manifested through voice or appear in a chat. What was unacknowledged, pushed away, becomes real.

I tell my students to get sleep before I close the session to begin the next period.

I ask my older students: *How should schools prepare students for the future?*

During the pandemic, this question feels awkward, loaded. Teaching credential programs have not prepared any of us for this: overheating computers, overwhelmed computer systems, faulty internet connections, compromised health, loss of life. All piled on top of poverty, including houselessness. Several students live in studios or garages with siblings and parents. The lucky ones have their own bedrooms in an apartment, maybe a house.

I'm not getting responses, so I ask again: *How should schools prepare students for the future?*

A brave student turns on her video and mic. It seems like she is sitting in a small backyard. Near the cement wall, there are trees. Her parents sit at a round table behind her. My student's voice competes with her parents' voluminous conversation. With my limited Spanish, I can tell they are engaged in a serious discussion. My student provides her one sentence reply, "Schools should prepare students for the future by teaching advanced computer skills." She smiles when she mutes her mic.

Another student's sibling cries in the background as she speaks, "Schools should prepare students for the future by teaching time management skills."

Another student sends a message. He needs to help a cousin in second grade with schoolwork.

When another student unmutes, I hear a female elementary school teacher in the background. Her colorful voice sounds like it belongs on *Sesame Street.*

Another student messages: *Miss, its too loud in here.*

Here is home. I don't ask what "it" refers to. Nor acknowledge the missing apostrophe.

I don't sleep at night.

I don't tell my students that I stay awake at night watching time pass. That at five in the morning I finally crash. I don't tell them that I refuse to watch the news because I fear for our futures, especially theirs, if Trump is elected again. I have no control over the president in office. I have no control over my dad's memory loss. I can't control whether my brother contracts COVID while delivering babies. I worry about my sister, who is also a teacher. She is scared that she might have been infected after delivering school supplies to students' apartments. A mother with COVID greeted her at the gate without a mask.

Like my students, I am afraid of losing my family.

With these layers, none of us are getting sufficient sleep.

I tell my students with their cameras on to turn them off.

I tell them that everything is passing.

My students close their eyes and ground their feet to earth.

I tell them they are part of earth: *This is where you belong.*

I tell them their bellies are glowing suns.

I tell them while we cannot always control reality, we can discover our inner power—because as Brown bodies we are resilient. With each inhale they imagine their inner light expanding. With each exhale they let go of one thought that no longer serves them: the self-doubt, the negative talk, the hurtful words they heard from someone else.

With each breath, we relax into our bodies.

Together, we learn to be compassionate with ourselves.

"MUTHA SIX," INK ON PAPER · JILLIAN DICKSON, 2020

Poetry | *E. Ethelbert Miller*

WHEN THE GAMES RETURN

———

—for Emily

When the games return
we will not hide behind the mask.
We will race out onto the field
to bask in fellowship and embrace
the sky, sun, and the four bases below.

There will be no fear in the air,
no sickness in the stands. There
will only be cheering and clapping
and a knowing that baseball is what
matters and our dreams are round
and hard and at times get caught
in our gloves.

When the tarp is lifted and rolled
back a sudden beauty will appear.
It will be the memories of what
we missed and what we love. It will
be baseball. It will be prayer.

———

Previously published in his book, *When Your Wife Has Tommy John Surgery and Other Baseball Stories*, City Point Press, 2021

"WASHINGTON," DIGITAL PAINTING · MICHAEL HOWER, 2020

WASTED

April 1, 2020

I've read so many memoirs written during unusual times, times of great famine, war, or plague, and it occurs to me that I should document what is happening now. I am currently on earth but in Federal Prison in Aliceville, Alabama. We are on full lockdown due to a global pandemic, the coronavirus. We live in a sheltered-from-the-outside place, and the officials took us gently down. Day by day, never telling us why, our movement on the compound lessened until we found ourselves stuck in our cells.

On the news people are dying. The entire thing is like a bad episode of South Park. The DOW dropped 974 points, and there are thousands of people dead in New York alone. Our president thrives on the vibration and cheer of the crowds. Thanks to social distancing, none may assemble and he seems withered.

I was able to keep a journal for the better part of April 1 to July 31, 2020. It should be noted that seven months have passed since I wrote that, and currently we are allowed out of our cells only three and a half hours a day and have just two hours of rec each week.

I've been watching a lot of news. The strange thing about federal prison is that there are eight big-screen TVs mounted on columns, and I can see three of them from my cell door. In hopes of learning about the progress of the pandemic, I was sucked into a political cesspool.

On the other end of my eight-by-ten-foot cell there is a window, and outside our compound it looks like a ghost town. Some 1,300 women are suddenly trapped in their rooms. I was one of the lucky ones because I live in the Honors Dorm, and the administration eventually, with great logic, turned our ninety-person dorm into frontline workers. Most prisons are run by the inmates; the officers merely lock and unlock doors but we "man" the departments. Food Service, Commissary, Facilities, Laundry, and Trash. Every department, such as Medical, the Lieutenant's office, and the compound grounds—all of this is cleaned and kept up by inmate orderlies. While 1,200 or more women were kept in their cells twenty-two to twenty-three hours a day (only allowed out to use the computer and shower or use the phone), I was and am still outside several mornings a week, tending the roses and watering the flower beds.

My heart aches each time I look up and see the sad, somber faces in the little windows, looking out as the seasons change. Women who are merely being warehoused, literally wasting away days.

———

Compound/Trash Orderly

> People too will vanish with the grasses!
> —Nunamoto no Muneyuki, ca. 930

———

Try to imagine our ghost town: cut lawn, red stripes directing traffic on the interconnecting roads of sidewalk, a concrete circle of buildings, my few small gardens but with no trees inside the farthest gate, about a mile out. One side could almost pass for a strip mall. The chow hall reminds me of a DMV in a pop-up neighborhood. There are three tall main buildings that could never be mistaken for anything other than prison. Each building holds about 450 women. Although we all come from different places on the globe, as of April 1, 2020, we now have this in common: the pandemic lockdown.

As a result of the pandemic and since the first day of April, our meals have been delivered to our units. At first they came through the bean shoot, a small slot cut in our doors, but for a while now, we have been able to come out and stand in line in the dayroom to get our breakfast, lunch, and dinner. Each morning the food service workers bring a cart with apples or bananas and crates of milk with paper bags containing cereal and/or a pastry or a (very bad for you) pop tart. The kitchen sends enough for us to have two cartons of milk (the elementary school size) and two pieces of fruit. The guard never allows this, almost always we are allowed just one. Please don't stop reading, thinking that this is a complaint about the lack of food. That is not what I am about—quite the opposite.

For nine months I have watched the news and seen people lined up all over America, hoping for free food. I have read articles in *Bloomberg Business* about the shortage of food and the poverty facing my fellow countrymen, about the schoolchildren who are going without school lunch. I have heard stories on NPR telling how one in six Americans are food deficient. And my heart is broken for them. I have known for a long time that we were a nation much like a house of cards and that all it takes is one bad turn to reveal our true hand.

And yet each morning I go out to work and on the corner of each unit there are boxes of untouched apples, crates of milk, and bags of cereal and pastries, set out as waste, to be compacted. I am not talking about a few every once in a while; I am talking about enough to feed a small community. As a matter of fact, I started keeping a count and, on average, there are about twelve crates of milk (and this is a few hours after they were served to us) and roughly three thousand apples. Every single day since April. I have spoken to numerous people. I wrote the kitchen administrator and offered logical solutions to the issue of waste. He literally asked if I were some kind of "tree hugger." (I should say that as I write this, I have seen smaller amounts of food on the corner in the past week, perhaps even by half, and I give credit to a certain woman who is in food service whom I have spoken to several times about the issue. But it could just be because we have had visitors.)

Meanwhile, in the words of the young environmentalist Greta Thunberg, "The emission curve, I am sorry but it's still rising. That curve is the only thing that we should look at. Every time we make a decision, we should ask ourselves, 'How will this decision affect that curve?'"

Each day at the trash compacter, I think of her words as I watch good food, plastic shampoo bottles, and a zillion other containers—soda pop cans and everything else that should be recycled—go into the machine.

For lunch and dinner, the kitchen delivers hot meals *served on Styrofoam shells*. We are talking about 2,600 Styrofoam shells each day. Later in the day, we gather those up and take them to the same compactor.

On the internet this is listed as a green prison.

The most interesting thing about the federal prison system is that there are ninety-two of them housing about 170,000 people. They are spread out across America, and they are all sitting on large plots of mowed lawn. I am reminded of a permaculture principle: it's never that you have too many grub worms, it's that you have a duck deficiency. The solution is always found in what is perceived as the problem. It's about the management, the system . . . the effort . . . efforts like using inmates to make cardboard food containers.

As a small child, when I was scolded for something, if I said, "I didn't mean to, Mommy," she always responded by saying, "but you didn't mean not to."

I know that in a perfect world we wouldn't have the largest prison population in the world, but it seems like we are adding insult to injury by having the most wasteful and poorly structured prisons imaginable. With all this land, the simple and logical solution is to garden these vast spaces, incorporating a bit of sustainability. I see this better utilization of land as a three-prong solution: (1) minimizing the trucks that deliver food from all over, food that isn't that great for us anyway, (2) giving us the ability to grow food for the poor communities that most prisons are nestled in, food that will eventually reduce the amount of pharmaceuticals and medical costs needed, (3) but mostly, teaching the captives how to till the earth, which after all is the best way to get better grounded and to grow your soul. They would realize a bit of personal success and learn community building.

———

Keeping Your Living Space Clean

> "Conservation is not merely a thing to be enshrined in outdoor museums, but a way of living on land."
>
> —Aldo Leopold, 1933

––––––

Last year I felt as if my time here was counting for something. My schedule was so different. I have always been one to stay busy and productive. I taught wellness and fitness classes in the Recreation Department. I taught adult continuing education classes and classes like conflict resolution and creative writing. I was able to spend several hours in the gym most mornings. I could forage the rec yard for dandelions to make my salad. I could walk the track with my headphones on and let my worries fall off by the quarter mile. I had a goal to finish my electrical vocational course (takes one year under normal conditions) and move on to a camp.

––––––

Now the prison is putting on a pony show that looks legit on paper but we are being warehoused, not reformed. I know that studies show that long periods of idleness and solitude amplify mental illness, and any doctor will tell you that a sedentary lifestyle has a laundry list of negative effects on a person's health. But here we all are.

In federal prison we are required to be "teamed" about every six months. At that time your case manager is supposed to talk to you about your "individual needs plan." It's like a program review. When the lock-in began and I realized that I was not going to be able to attend classes or teach, I enrolled in a college correspondence course (Construction Management). I am able to make payments of thirty seven dollars a month until nearly a thousand dollars is paid for a nonaccredited vocational, paper-based course. I am fortunate to have this sort of advantage.

Yet still, in my case manager's haste, my team papers read as follows:

PROGRESS SINCE LAST REVIEW *Unable to fully successfully program at this time due to Covid-19. Will review at next team and determine if programming is obtainable. At that time a new goal will be given. You should be focusing on your mental health and keeping your living space clean.*

I do recognize that we are not the only ones sitting around. I am fully aware that America has been sheltered in place—or perhaps they were not and that is why now December 7, as I write this, the news is reporting that an American dies every minute.

History shows us again and again how the powerful people prioritize profit over human life. This current pandemic is no exception. The American government passed the CARES Act, which included an out for "at-risk inmates." Across America prisons were allowed to send people home on an ankle monitor. I read an extensive article in *Bloomberg Business* about the companies that were competing to provide those ankle monitors, driving the cost up. Yes, even in a global pandemic there are those who find a way to profit from the most disenfranchised. Michael Cohen, the former president's lawyer, was released after just thirteen months of his three-year sentence, but my friend Joyce had a very different experience.

Joyce is seventy-two and meets several of the CDC markers: she is obese, over sixty, has high blood pressure, and takes ACE inhibitors; she has asthma and sleeps with a CPAP machine for sleep apnea. In the first phase of the lock-in, the unit team had her sign papers for home confinement. They contacted her family, and each week they returned with more papers to sign. The weeks went by, four weeks, six weeks, eight weeks—nothing. One of the things I love the most about Ms. Joyce is that she always met you with a smile. She has a thirty-year sentence like me, and she has always remained optimistic, cheerful, and positive.

One day they told her it was all a mistake—she wouldn't be able to go home. After hearing that, she began to look haggard and stressed. Each day she seemed to be digressing. Finally they pulled her out and took her to quarantine and then to camp. Hopefully they will be more kind to her wherever she ends up.

———

In the Space Where I Was Meant to Be

"Our prison population, in fact, is now the biggest in the history of human civilization. There are more people in the United States either on parole or in jail today (around 6 million total) than there were where at any time in Stalin's gulags. For a country founded on the idea that rights are inalienable and inherent from birth, we've developed a high tolerance for conditional rights. Obsessed with success and wealth and despising failure and poverty, our society is systematically dividing the population into winners and losers, using institutions like the courts to speed the process."

—Matt Taibbi, *The Divide: American Injustice in the Age of the Wealth Gap*

———

Who flips the bill for my incarceration? If I am not mistaken, the tax-payers of America are paying for these 170,000 federal inmates. For my sentence of thirty years—a one-count conspiracy for using drugs for two years, selling small amounts of drugs to support my habit when I started running out of money and ultimately for introducing one of my beaus to a guy whom he later bought drugs from—you will pay $1.8 million to house me. And that is if I somehow beat the odds eating the food here and don't need medical attention as I age from fifty to seventy-five. And then there is the cost of caring for my mother, who will not have me there to help her in her old age. My nieces won't have me there to teach them all of the valuable lessons I have learned, and any number of people will feel the difference of my absence. You see I may be deemed a horrible person by the judge and prosecutor, but my crime had only one direct victim and that was me, and I left a gap of goodness in the space where I was meant to be.

I remember standing in front of the judge, my life in shambles, pouring my heart out to him, completely misunderstanding what it means to be a judge in America, . . . and in response he shamed me for wasting his time, for wasting the taxpayers' money. How dare I take up the space to ruin my life and stand before him. And yet, here I am, day after pandemic day, watching the big flat-screen through my twenty-foot-by-five-inch window, and every single day the newsman reports another frivolous lawsuit filed in another court . . . our democracy laying waste.

———

Memorial Day 2020

Everything is completely surreal. Not surreal like a Salvador Dali or a trip through the forest on shrooms . . . no, like dystopian style. Late last night I saw a woman on television, interviewing #45. With each calmly posed question, the answers literally dropped my jaw. She continued to smile and gulp down the insanity before moving on to the next question. A chill ran down my spine. There is, as sure as I am sitting here, still locked in my room twenty-one hours a day—a global pandemic going on, people all over the world are marching for equality in the streets, the fires in the west are burning something like four football fields of forest every hour and the basic conversation of the interview was more like, "I have done the best job ever!" History and democracy may soon be erased and all we'll be left with are lies. The most surreal aspect for me is that I am in federal prison for the next twenty-five years and yet I am terribly afraid for everyone else's freedom.

Never were these words of Greta Thunberg more true. In her essay "The Crisis Is Already Here," published in *Lapham's Quarterly*, she writes:

We have to start treating the crisis like a crisis, and act even if we don't have all the solutions.

"That is still not an answer," you say.

Then we start talking about circular economy and rewilding nature and the need for a just transition. Then you don't understand what we are talking about.

We say that all those solutions needed are not known to anyone and therefore we must unite behind the science and find them together along the way. But you do not listen to that because those answers are for solving a crisis that most of you don't fully understand. Or don't want to understand.

You don't listen to the science, because you are only interested in solutions that will enable you to carry on like before. Like now. And those answers don't exist anymore because you did not act in time.

When I read these words, I was blown away by the relevance of this moment. This could be talking about the Black Lives Matter movement or the inability to deal with this pandemic or the climate crisis or even mass incarceration.

At the beginning of the lock-in, something quite magical happened to me. A few months before the pandemic, my cousin had placed a simple add on Write-a-Prisoner. Day after lonely day, as I was shut in my room for all but one to three hours a day, letters started flooding in. The letters were mostly from young women, students, artists, teachers from all over the world! Just when I needed to feel alive and relevant, this outpouring of love and understanding arrived. What if this were part of the "rewilding." An idea of love and forgiveness and second chances. My mother always says, "People will forget your name, forget your face, but they will never forget how you made them feel."

Anyone who has ever planted a garden knows the basic and simple principles of life and of this earth; you plant a seed and water it, nurture it . . . and it grows until little by little, one day it's a plant. And this is true of anything. We are tomorrow what we plant today. We have to start working together if we want our children, our grandchildren and our nieces to be healthy and have a place to learn and roam, to have a space to grow—a life worth living.

August 20, 2020

To whom it may Concern: Greetings.!!

I am writing this letter to present you with my poem INFECTION COVID-19 as part of my submission as a Latino prisoner who has been incarcerated since May-1971.

I am a Cuban-American who left Cuba on July 30, 1966. My mother, a simple and Native Cuba; My father a soldier in the cuban army: I was the eldest son of a family in turmoil during the Cuban rebellion of 1959.

With the exception of my two daughters, all my family has died during my incarceration. During my Journey here I was contaminated with Tuberculosis and spent one year in treatment. At my age I also an affected by high blood pressure, sleep apnea and short of breath.

The poem is a personal message that deals with my medical concerns, and the environmental phenomenun that we as humans are encountering with the pandemic, killing thousands of people at a time of civil crisis in America, fires in California and unpredictable weather conditions.

My trials and tribulations are expressed in the language of a man who has never given up hope. My determination to be free,

—————— OVER —→

"IMAGE OF FIRST PAGE OF LETTER," PHOTOGRAPH
LUIS PEREZ, 2020

my positive attitude, my incessant fight
for human rights, my care for Global environment, will strike a thought-provoking
chord in the hearts of many readers.

I am also a self promotu writer
who already publ'sh'd two books:

Depatriado
Man without Country

And Abnormal Footprint.

I Sincerely hope that you publish my
poem on yours Anthology.

Sincerely yours,
One Love in the struggle.

Luis P. Perez

"IMAGE OF SECOND PAGE OF LETTER," PHOTOGRAPH
LUIS PEREZ, 2020

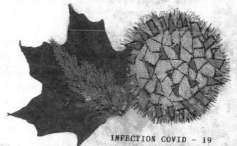

INFECTION COVID - 19

The trees are not indifferent,
he can't be contaminated,
but from the roots,
the trees think like being chopped
to become the walls of someone's house.

We think different when death is close.
Slowly the poison of the coronavirus,
while the roots of nature have been
diverged from nature's first green and
gold to the darkest evening of the year.

The contamination can't infect
my sovereign spirit.
I got caught between the heaves of storm
and surviving the death force.

Incarceration until you dead,
that is my other COVID-19.
Rivers of human souls, opened the coffins
and set them all free by faith.
Life and hope came as in tears,
while the country is crying waiting for
the midnight rain of love to fall.

Can I see the sun again?
Can I be touched by the rain and the air?
Drops of sweat are splashing on the ground,
waiting for the rain stop, so one day
I would be free again,
that is the feeling of nature
reflecting in a human soul.

Neither the fresh air
or being touched by
sun, the double qua-
rantene is saving my
life now, so that
I can die later.

Covid-19 does not
have compassion for
me, neither the
government that is
holding me in.

Millions of sick people
and thounsands alreay
dead - while cold cell
doors are traping me
in the dark. - I am
bleeding slowly on papers
where I am writing in
blood - coughing my breath.

The drezzling of rain
continues to fall,
surfing the virus again?
Oh my GOD,
riverbeds of justice
for us all over again.

IT is my personal message
from the leaf of the tree.

We need to make changes in the environment. The human race is
served with a terrible pandamic to remind us all that we should
look at the Globan Climate with the seriousness it demands. It
is not for our future generation to correct the errors, it is
for us to work on humanity's needs.

Luis Perez W33937
NCCI / - GARDNER STATE PRISON

August 20, 2020

"INFECTION COVID-19," PHOTOGRAPH OF POEM
LUIS PEREZ, 2020

THIS IS NOT THE END OF THE WORLD

———

In dreams, I am slowly and methodically beating a man
senseless. Or trying to. We all are, all the time. I write the best
love poems to the sound
of bird calls. Only when I'm far away
can I imagine you, breathing quietly
and dreaming. Moving your body a bit. You told me your father
would like me with a firm handshake, our mighty paws woven
    together
like men. At the last moment meeting him my palm maneuvered
like a plane into a building. But this is not the end
of the world. I will walk further into the music of a few birds and
    their mating
calls to one another before the morning storm. I will forever jog
toward that boy on the park path jumping into puddles
and out of them as if traversing hundreds of feet of oceans re-
    entering the sky
and earth. I will always lose, become suddenly
like a bullet fired underwater. The wind will work hard
at my spine. The joy will make my throat burn with the taste
of metal. Of my mother's throat. Only then will I raise my arms
the way runners do at the end of a marathon. The way dancers
    do at the end
of dances. My lips working silently. To let go
a memory of my father. The sole time his hand rose and fell
he struck me. I was four. Through all this, I've learned only that
    distance
is impossible. At the end of the world, my hands and my body

will become limp and feverish. My fist languid
as a flower. It will brush against the other man's chin. At the end
of the world,
I will always be saving somebody. And how wonderful
that the first time I met your father, my fingers rested on the tops
of his like a lady's
at a ball asking politely for a dance.

Previously published in *Bluestem Magazine*

TOUCH SCREEN

———

It's almost 9 a.m. on a Saturday morning in November, and rain is pelting the windows. Just as well, since I am spending this morning at a board retreat. I pull a red stole over my nightgown, finger lipstick on for some color, but not too much to look made-up, pull unbrushed hair in a ponytail, grab a mug of coffee, and sit in front of my laptop.

Faces pop up like portraits in a gallery. I miss galleries. What is it about flyaway hairs on Zoom that are invisible in real life? Everyone always comes on and starts to smooth their fly-aways, the novices usually smoothing down the opposite side of their heads . . . Hello people, we are nine months into this . . .

I should not have binge-watched the *Queen's Gambit* till 4:30 a.m. Nor drunk glasses of red wine, like I was keeping up with Beth Harmon.

The board chair calls the meeting to order. First agenda item is to meet the new board member. "I won't repeat Julian's stellar profile, you all have seen it. Julian, we all welcome you to our board." I forgot his profile was in an email several months ago. A lawyer, I recall, wondering why we're adding K Street types who cozy up to whoever pays the bill. And since when do lawyers care about poor kids getting an arts education? My vote was outnumbered. Guess sometimes it's about who brings in the bucks on these nonprofit boards.

"Thanks for inviting me to join, it's an honor. I've always admired this organization." I look up from my coffee mug to see the source of this baritone voice. His dark hair is pulled back in a ponytail. Silvering at the temples. More artist than lawyer. Around my age, somewhere in the fifties, I guess.

The board chair screen-shares a list of the committees and calls on the chairs to introduce each one, starting with me. I launch into how the

Strategic Planning Committee will design the next five-year plan, how we pivoted ("word of the year ha ha") from in-person to online and may go hybrid in a post-COVID era, what funding challenges we expect, but how we've redoubled our commitment to low-income youth.

Julian has an emoji clap in his rectangle when I finish.

After everyone has introduced their committee, the chair asks Julian to choose one to serve on. Feels like a beauty contest. He picks mine. Speaking of which, I check my settings and quickly hit "touch up my appearance."

Next we go into breakout groups to talk about why we serve on the board as part of the "bonding/renewing our commitment" portion of the agenda. I love breakouts, such intimate spaces and the excitement of discovering who the algorithm bundles me with. *Seriously? Am pathetic . . .*

Chris, Sandy, me, . . . and Julian are in breakout group number 4. Chris says blah blah. Sandy says blah blah. I say more blah. Julian talks about his pro bono work representing DACA kids. He was a theater major before law school, stills acts in small theaters in New York. He's moving to DC in four months, thinking he can teach an acting or playwriting class to the kids in the program. I've always loved the name Julian. Like Julian Barnes . . . We're buffered back to plenary.

An hour later, the chat box lights up. I love such distractions, especially when talking audits and fundraising plans. It's a private message. From Julian. "Are you free to catch me up before the next SPC meet?"

"Sure. And welcome."

"Thanks. And red becomes you."

Am about to respond, "and blue, you," what if I hit "message everyone" by mistake—or, can the host read all the private chats too? This session is being recorded.

So I just look at him and our eyes lock. Can we both be looking straight into the camera above everyone's faces à la *Zoom-training tips* at the same time? He raises an eyebrow. And they say you can't read cues in Zoom. I say those people can't read cues period. I quickly look away in case the whole room sees us seeing us.

The retreat is over. We all wave, and like apparitions, one by one, we disappear, the remaining growing larger and larger as each human-in-a-rectangle departs.

My inbox has a Zoom calendar invite for 5 p.m. in the evening. I accept.

———

I'm wearing a black dress. Even put on high heels. Visibly red lipstick. Scheduled a Zoom meeting at 4:50 p.m. (participant 1) to check myself on video, smooth down any fly-aways in advance. I pour myself a glass of red wine, and hit his Zoom link at 5:07 p.m., to be not too eager. He's there in a denim jacket over a black T-shirt. His face fills the screen, and his eyes are a warm brown. There's music playing.

"Cheese Cake," I say. "My favorite piece of Dexter Gordon's."

He smiles a hello, and raises his glass to the screen. I do the same, "Clink. Cheers."

"Black becomes you too," he says. "But then, just about any color would, I think."

"So what did you think of the retreat?" I ask. I'm a little nervous. Have been on one Bumble date since my friend Jill forced me to sign up last month.

He was saying he enjoyed it, everyone was so welcoming, so committed.

"My husband used to play the sax," I interrupt. "This piece, especially."

He raises that same eyebrow. "He stopped playing?"

"I lost him. Two years ago. Damn cancer."

We both sip quietly. And the music stops.

"I'm not used to . . . have not been on a date, well only one earlier this month, and it wasn't great, and my friend made me sign up for one of these dating sites, said I can't mourn forever, although sorry, this is not really a date, although it's kind of feeling like one and . . . sorry, feel like I am babbling which I—"

"He was a very lucky guy to have been with you for . . . how many years?"

"Twenty-eight. We met when we were in college. I have two grown sons. But tell me about you."

"She left me for someone else, after twenty years together. A rich lawyer, way richer than a civil rights kind of lawyer. We have a daughter who lives in Seattle."

How much more could his eyes say? They are luminous on my screen.

"So, you're into strategic planning?"

He laughs. "Bad deflection. More like I plan strategically." He plays more music.

"Wonderful. Another favorite. Grover Washington—*Winelight*."

We gaze at each other.

"Can I kiss you?" he leans in close.

I do too. We kiss. It's called a touch screen after all.

Previously published in *Bloom*

NOTES

Epigraph from Catherine Belling, "Overwhelming the Medium: Fiction and the Trauma of Pandemic Influenza in 1918," *Literature and Medicine* 28, no. 1 (Spring 2009): 55–81, https://muse.jhu.edu/issue/19755.

The following titles were derived from these contributors' works:

Fear: "It lives in droplets"—Frances Ogamba

Distance: "As we moan into the phone"—John Cuetara

Mask: "A parachute that catches my breath"—Stephanie Lenox

Labor: "Warnings on the floor"—Ranney Campbell

Sickness: "My stomach charlie-horsed"—Brett L. Massey

Grief: "Interjected like a comma"—Jen Karetnick

Survival: "Remember every surface you touch"—Rosalie Hendon

Justice and Reckoning: "Colonial co-morbidities"—Ahimsa Timoteo Bodhrán

Environment and Place: "Let the river turn the stone"—Caroline Furr

Hope: "Beyond sorrow there's a gardenia tree"—Deborah "Deby" Rodriguez

CONTRIBUTORS

Rasha Abdulhadi is a queer Palestinian Southerner whose work has been anthologized in *Halal if You Hear Me*, *Super Stoked*, and *Luminescent Threads: Connections to Octavia Butler*. They edit fiction at *Strange Horizons* and are a member of Justice for Muslims Collective, the Radius of Arab American Writers, and Alternate ROOTS. Their chapbook, *who is owed springtime*, is forthcoming from Neon Hemlock Press.

Faiza Anum is a poet and educator from Lahore, Pakistan. She has published poems in *The Pinch Journal*, *The Stonecoast Review*, *Transnational Literature*, *Illumen* (Alban Lake Publications), *Stoneboat Literary Journal*, *Antinarrative Poetry Journal*, *The Ghazal Page*, *Eastern Structures*, *The Lake*, *Cadence* (Clarendon House Books), and elsewhere. Her poem "Travelling Tales" was a finalist for Open Road Review Poetry Prize in 2015. She teaches English at University of South Asia, Lahore.

Monserrat Escobar Arteaga is a DACA student, COVID-19 survivor, and was a COVID-19 contact tracer from July 2020 to April 2021. She migrated to America from Mexico in 2005. She is currently an upcoming senior at Trevecca University where she majors in psychology with a minor in biology. She is the vice president of FUTURO and is on the board of directors for the nonprofit Southern Word.

Joan E. Bauer is the author of *The Almost Sound of Drowning* (Main Street Rag, 2008) and *The Camera Artist* (Turning Point, 2021). She was born in California in 1947, worked for some years as a teacher and counselor, and now lives mostly in Pittsburgh, where she co-hosts and curates the Hemingway's Summer Poetry Series with Kristofer Collins. She can be found on Twitter at @Joan_E_Bauer.

Thomas Beckwith holds a master of arts in higher education from the University of Arizona as well as master of public administration from Florida Gulf Coast University. He also holds a bachelor of arts in English with a concentration in creative writing from Virginia Tech. NACADA recently selected Thomas as one of the ten Emerging Leaders for 2021–23. Beckwith enjoys watching movies and sports and traveling throughout the United States.

Alice Benson lives in Wisconsin with her wife and their two dogs. She discovered writing as a passion in the third act of her life and spends much of her time in pursuit of metaphors. The story contained in this anthology reflects a few of her thoughts, fears, and experiences during this pandemic. Alice recently retired from a job in a human services field. For more information, visit her website at www.alicebensonauthor.com.

Christopher Blackwell is incarcerated at the Washington Correction Center in Shelton, Washington, and is working toward publishing a book on solitary confinement. His writing has been published by the *Washington Post*, *BuzzFeed*, *Jewish Currents*, *INSIDER*, and many other publications. He is serving a forty-five-year sentence. Follow Christopher on Twitter @ChrisWBlackwell.

Celeste Blair is currently serving 360 months for a one-count conspiracy to possess a controlled substance. She has been an artist all her life. Stripped of paint, she used written words to purge her soul and heart and sinew. If she were painting the social scene around her, there would be few smiling faces, as the war on drugs has taken mothers from their children. A self-portrait should reveal an aging woman, young at heart and still hopeful of a good next chapter.

Nathan Blalock is an urban sci-fi writer who enjoys taking readers on trips. Although he has written in other genres, painting the picture for the reader is always important. Born in Michigan, Nathan grew up absorbing science fiction, TV, movie boom, and role-playing video games. Now in California, those elements keep his writing fresh and inviting.

Mix in real urban issues and global problems, and, well, you get the pictures.

Ahimsa Timoteo Bodhrán is a member of the CantoMundo, Macondo, VONA, RAWI, and Lambda Literary communities. A Tulsa Artist Fellow and National Endowment for the Arts Fellow, he is the author of *Archipiélagos*; *Antes y después del Bronx: Lenapehoking*; and *South Bronx Breathing Lessons*; editor of the global queer Indigenous issue of *Yellow Medicine Review: A Journal of Indigenous Literature, Art, and Thought*; and coeditor of the Native dance/movement/performance issue of *Movement Research Performance Journal*.

Phrieda Bogere has written poetry for years before making the decision to share her work with a wider audience. Her work has been featured in *Brave Voices Magazine*, *The Beautiful Space*, *Writing in a Woman's Voice*, and other publications. When she isn't writing, she loves exercising and getting lost in a good book.

Michele Bombardier's debut collection, *What We Do*, was a Washington Book Award finalist. Her work has appeared in *Alaska Quarterly Review*, *Atlanta Review*, *Parabola*, *Bellevue Literary Review*, and many others. She is a Hedgebrook and Mineral School fellow and the founder of Fishplate Poetry. She earned an MFA in poetry from Pacific University and lives on an island in Puget Sound.

Mark Brazaitis is the author of eight books, including *The River of Lost Voices: Stories from Guatemala*, winner of the 1998 Iowa Short Fiction Award, and *The Incurables*, winner of the 2012 Richard Sullivan Prize. His stories, essays, and poems have appeared in *Ploughshares*, *The Sun*, *Witness*, *Michigan Quarterly Review*, and elsewhere. A former Peace Corps volunteer and technical trainer, he is a professor of English at West Virginia University.

Maya Lear Brewer is the daughter of a Dutch Indonesian immigrant mother and an American father. She is a freelance writer, an ESOL teacher, and an emerging creative nonfiction writer. As a writer, Brewer enjoys exploring her heritage, her life as a child from a divorced family and its intersection with raising her own five children, and the world at large. "We Are Family" is her first published creative nonfiction essay. Connect with her @MayaBrewwrites.

Ranney Campbell is a former journalist and earned an MFA in fiction from the University of Missouri at St. Louis. Her poetry has been published in *Misfit Magazine*, *Shark Reef*, *Haight Ashbury Literary Journal*, and others, and her chapbook, *Pimp*, is published by Arroyo Seco Press.

Yuan Changming coedits *Poetry Pacific* with Allen Yuan at http://poetry pacific.blogspot.ca. Credits include eleven Pushcart nominations, ten chapbooks, and appearances in *Best of the Best Canadian Poetry* (2008–2017) and *BestNewPoemsOnline*, among 1,839 other literary outlets, across forty-six countries. Recently, Yuan served on the jury for Canada's 44th National Magazine Awards (English poetry category).

Alyce Copeland is bipolar. She grew up in an abusive family and then married a combination of her bipolar father and domineering mother. By sixty, she lived alone for the first time and was raped by a neighbor. His charges were dropped as she was considered an unreliable witness due to her mental illness. When someone else got too close, she shot him (he survived). Her sentence: eighteen years. What she's learned in prison? The majority of incarcerated women have the same background.

Ilaria Cortesi is a self-taught digital artist based in Shanghai, China. She started making analog collages at a young age and, seeking a creative outlet, rediscovered this art form while juggling a full-time office job and single parenthood. Since then, she has adopted digital collage and illustration as a means of personal and social liberation and as a critical lens to look at stereotypical views and representations of society and individuals. https://www.behance.net/ilariac.

Judea Costes (she/they) is a photographer and singer/songwriter. Currently their photo work explores the relationships and tensions created by dichotomies within an image—illumination and shadow, life and decay, organic and inorganic, for example—and how these dichotomies together create portals to individual and unique worlds of their own. Judea was born to Jamaican and Filipinx parents in Queens, New York, and still resides there to this day.

John Cuetara is a published poet, short story writer, and psychologist who lives with his wife on the banks of the Mystic Lakes in West Medford, Massachusetts. His poems and stories have appeared in a dozen literary quarterlies and in three collections of his own work. Many years ago he studied with Bernard Malamud and John Gardner at Bennington College in Vermont.

Roan Davis is a massage therapist by trade. She has a clientele of first responders and has been experiencing compassion burnout for months now, even as she tries to make it a point to give them the tender care they need to get them back on their feet. The poem "White." was inspired by an experience that happened right before lockdown when her clientele and work were impacted directly because of her Asian heritage. Roan lives in West Virginia.

Deidra Suwanee Dees, EdD, /family descend from *Hotvlkvlke* (Wind Clan) following Muscogee stompdance traditions. Chapbook author of *Vision Lines: Native American Decolonizing Literature* (TA Publications, 2004), she serves as director/tribal archivist at the Poarch Band of Creek Indians whose strong leadership is safely guiding the community through COVID-19. She teaches Native American Studies at the University of South Alabama, Tribally sponsored. A Cornell and Harvard graduate, she works on equity for the underrepresented. *Heleswv heres, mvto.*

Deborah DeNicola has written seven books, most recently *The Impossible*, which won the poetry competition at the Los Angeles Book Festival,

Original Human, and her memoir, *The Future That Brought Her Here*. She edited the anthology *Orpheus and Company: Contemporary Poems on Greek Mythology* (University Press of New England). Previous books include *Where Divinity Begins* and four chapbooks, two of which were award winners. Among other awards, she was also awarded an Individual Artist's NEA grant.

Kim Denning is a Latina writer whose inspiration draws from growing up in El Paso, Texas, but having lived her adult life in the Austin area. Her writing is shaped by cultural experiences gifted by her Mexican American mother and Texas cowboy father. Kim is a community organizer and clinical assistant professor in the UTeach-Liberal Arts program at the University of Texas at Austin, where she teaches emerging teachers how to inspire bigger and more just dents in the universe.

Jillian Dickson hails from a downtown-less town called Darien in the great state of Illinois. She has traveled the world with a southern gent and loves the smell of her daughter's yogurt-encrusted hair. Jillian received her BFA from Bradley University in 2005 and her MFA from Clemson University in 2007. Jillian is a visiting assistant professor in drawing and painting at Alma College in Michigan.

donnarkevic lives in Buckhannon, West Virginia and holds an MFA from National University. Recent work has or will appear in *Street Cake*, *Neologism Poetry Journal*, and *Solum Literary Press*.

Eric Ebers, born in 1987, fell into substance abuse at an early age, which led to his incarceration. In prison, he discovered he had a voice capable of reaching the masses. Outside of working and going to college, he works on writing and performing spoken-word poetry. He currently has seven deeply compelling pieces to his name that he plans to share with the world in hopes of healing "the broken."

Vanessa Chica Ferreira is a New York City educator, poet, playwright, fat activist, poetry editor for the Ice Colony, and founder of theWORDbox.

A featured poet at various events throughout New York City, she co-wrote and performed in a three-woman play titled *Live Big Girl*, which debuted at the National Black Theatre. Her work has been published in the *BX Files*, *The Abuela Stories Project*, *The Acentos Review*, and *Great Weather for Media*. For more information, visit www.vanessachica.com.

Liseli A. Fitzpatrick, PhD, is a Trinidadian poet and professor of African cosmologies and sacred ontologies at Wellesley College, Massachusetts. Her penchant for poetry is driven by her desire to effect emancipatory change in the co-creation of an equitable, just, and breathable world. Her work has appeared or is forthcoming in *About Place Journal*, *Chicken Soup for the Soul: I'm Speaking Now*, *A (Re)Turn to the African Girl: (Re)Defining African Girlhood Studies* edited collection, and *Feminists Speak Whiteness Anthology*. In 2019 she was a Furious Flower Poetry Center Fellow.

Michael Fox is an artist currently incarcerated in Stockton, California. He is part of the Freedom through Art Collective. He hopes his work brings a smile to someone's face.

Caroline Furr began professional and personal life in Texas, then completed an MA in sculpture in Los Angeles. She has worked in museums and galleries, sometimes as a founder and director, and has painted sets for TV and film. When living in Barcelona, she began writing, and in Philadelphia, she took on surface and interior design. More at https://carolinefurr.com and @carolinefurrdesign.art (Instagram).

Robbie Gamble's poems and essays have appeared in the *Atlanta Review*, *RHINO*, *Rust + Moth*, *Scoundrel Time*, and *Tahoma Literary Review*. He was a Peter Taylor Fellow in creative nonfiction at the Kenyon Summer Writers Workshop and winner of the 2017 *Carve* poetry prize. He worked for twenty years as a nurse practitioner with Boston Health Care for the Homeless Program, and now divides his time between Boston and Vermont.

Veronica Scharf Garcia grew up overseas in South America, Africa, the Middle East, and Europe. She continues her itinerant life now in Europe.

California was her last home base, three years ago. She has exhibited her art extensively in the United States and Peru and was awarded several artist residencies. This work, "Manibus," is part of a photographic collage series made in Bergamo, Italy, during the nationwide lockdown in February 2020. https://www.instagram.com/verogoart/

Kasha Martin Gauthier lives outside Boston with her family. A member of the Workshop for Publishing Poets, Kasha's poetry is informed by her family dynamics, upbringing in New Hampshire, and careers in business and cybersecurity. Kasha's work is forthcoming or has recently appeared in *The Healing Muse, Slipstream, Main Street Rag, Constellations*, and *Soundings East*.

Adam J. Gellings is a writer and instructor from Columbus, Ohio. His previous work has appeared in *DIALOGIST, The Louisville Review, Willow Springs*, and elsewhere. He currently teaches at Columbus College of Art and Design.

Katy Giebenhain is the author of *Sharps Cabaret* (Mercer University Press). Her creative writing MPhil is from University of South Wales (Glamorgan). She is a member of her local DFA Healthcare Task Force and is particularly interested in improving access to essential medicines. Her poems have appeared in *The Examined Life Journal, The Arkansas Review, New Welsh Review, Appalachian Journal*, and elsewhere.

Laura Glenn's book of poems, *I Can't Say I'm Lost*, was published by FootHills, her chapbook *When the Ice Melts*, by Finishing Line. Her poems have appeared in many journals, including *Boulevard, Cortland Review, Epoch, Green Mountains Review, Hotel Amerika*, and *Poetry*, as well as in anthologies. She has completed another book of poems and a chapbook of pandemic poems. Also a visual artist, she lives in Ithaca, New York, and works as a freelance copy editor.

Gloria Goguen is a New England–based visual artist exploring classical forms of botanical art. In the spring of 2020, COVID-19 prevented the public viewing of her first major solo exhibit, "Botanical Dreams," which was ready to open just days before the pandemic sparked widespread closures. Since then, she spent time acquiring a variety of new techniques including intaglio printing, as in this example—"Clematis." Gloria is a member of the American Society of Botanical Artists.

Joan Goodreau's recent works include *Where to Now?*, memoir *Strangers Together: How My Son's Autism Changed My Life*, and *Another Secret Shared and Other Poems*. Her writing has appeared in numerous anthologies, periodicals, and reviews. She has been awarded a residency in the Hedgebrook Writers program. Joan's experience as a special education teacher and program specialist allows her to see the puzzle of autism from both the perspective of a parent and a professional.

Ben Gunsberg is an associate professor of English at Utah State University. His poems appear in numerous literary magazines, including *Poetry Daily*, *DIAGRAM*, and *Mid-American Review*. The author of the poetry collection *Welcome, Dangerous Life* and the chapbook *Rhapsodies with Portraits*, his poetry has won awards from the University of Michigan Hopwood Center and the Utah Division of Arts and Museums. He lives in Logan, Utah, at the foot of the Bear River Mountains.

Jameka Hartley, PhD, is an interdisciplinary Black feminist poet and scholar. She is an assistant professor of women and gender studies in the Department of History, Philosophy, and Social Sciences at Rhode Island School of Design. Her work centers on issues of Black motherhood, popular cultural representations of Black women, child to adult outcomes, and stigma. Her simultaneous identities of being a daughter and a mother shape both her life and her scholarship.

Rosalie Hendon is an environmental planner living in Columbus, Ohio, with her new husband and many house plants. She started a virtual poetry group during quarantine that has collectively written over two hundred poems. Her work is published in *Change Seven*, *Planisphere Q*,

Call Me [Brackets], *Entropy*, and *Pollux*. Rosalie is inspired by ecology, relationships, and stories passed down through generations.

Noe Hernandez was born in Mexico and migrated to New York as a child. He was an average student, usually in anime or drama club, laughing and talking with just about anyone. He wears his heart on his sleeve and dislikes seeing people in pain. Although unsure of his dream job, he always yearned to help people. Noe discovered that he is a spiritual healer and is also studying to become a massage therapist.

Joan Hofmann, professor emerita at the University of Saint Joseph, serves on the Riverwood Poetry Board, and was first poet laureate of Canton, Connecticut. Author of three chapbooks, *Coming Back, Alive,* and *Alive, Too,* her poems are published or forthcoming in *Forgotten Women, Waking Up to the Earth, Concho River Review, Tiger Moth Review, Wild Word, Connecticut River Review, Buddhist Poetry Review, Bird's Thumb, The Wayfarer, Dillydoun Review, Canary, SLANT,* and *Plainsongs.*

Michael Hower is an artist and photographer from central Pennsylvania. His work focuses on historical themes. He photographs abandoned places, depicting human objects and structures in modified environments now devoid of human activity. His artwork has appeared in galleries, museums, and publications around the country.

Diego Islas is a twenty-nine-year-old athletic man who was born in Chicago and raised in Houston. Diego is an outgoing, eccentric individual as well as a medic, roughneck, handyman, Catholic, motivator, and a hard-working, kind soul. He is also the father of an awesome son. He credits his work ethic to his grandfather with whom he spent many summers working on the ranch. Diego's something like a trap cowboy.

Peter Joel lives in Mindelo, Cape Verde. Born in the United States, he has lived and worked on three continents and traveled to over fifty countries. Peter wrote his first haiku at age eleven, after discovering the poems in the school library. Since then, he has been writing haiku, limericks, lyric poems, and light verse for his own amusement and that of friends and family.

Lukpata Lomba Joseph resides in Port Harcourt, Nigeria. He is a computer programming instructor by day and a poet by night. His work has previously appeared in the *Tipton Poetry Journal*, Jacar Press's *One*, *South Florida Poetry Journal*, *Euphemism Journal*, *Caustic Frolic*, *Agbowo Magazine*, *Dreich*, and elsewhere. Lukpata's work has been nominated for the Best of the Net award. Find him at facebook /lukpata.joseph.9.

Miami-based poet, writer, and journalist **Jen Karetnick's** fourth full-length book of poems is *The Burning Where Breath Used to Be* (David Robert Books, 2020), an Eric Hoffer Poetry Category Finalist and a Kops-Fetherling Honorable Mention. She is also the author of the poetry collection *Hunger Until It's Pain* (Salmon Poetry, 2023) and eighteen other books. Cofounder and managing editor of *SWWIM Every Day*, she has award-winning work appearing widely. See https://jkaretnick.com.

Lavinia Kumar's latest books are *Hear Ye, Hear Ye: Women*, *Women: Soldiers, Spies of Revolutionary and Civil Wars*, *No Longer Silent: The Silk and Iron of Women Scientists*, and *Beauty. Salon. Art.* Her poems range from science to surreal, history, and the everyday. Latest or upcoming poems are in *River Heron's Review* special compilation, *Poems for Now*, *Hole in the Head Review*, *Decolonial Passage*, *Superpresent.com*, and *SurVision*. Her website is laviniakumar.net.

Danielle Lauren is an unrepresented writer from Chicago. Danielle's fiction has been published in *CC&D Magazine* (2020) and she has an MA in journalism from Indiana University Bloomington. A former trade journalist, Danielle left the field to focus on her creative writing five years ago. She has since launched a wine blog and written a collection of short stories. She's currently writing a novel.

Stephanie Lenox is the author of two poetry collections, *The Business*, winner of the 2015 Colorado Prize for Poetry, and *Congress of Strange People*. During the pandemic, she created the quarantina, a poetic prose form of forty words exactly that isolates and expresses an experience through extreme restriction. She is an enrolled member of the Pokagon Band of Potawatomi and a student of Bodwéwadmimwen, the language of her ancestors. She lives in Salem, Oregon, where she works for Chemeketa Community College.

Robert J. Levy's work has appeared in *Paris Review, Poetry, Kenyon Review, Southern Review, Georgia Review, Gettysburg Review, Threepenny Review, North American Review, Southwest Review, Alaska Quarterly Review, Michigan Quarterly Review, Prairie Schooner, River Styx, Boulevard*, and elsewhere. His fourth full-length collection, *Beauty and Forfeiture*, was published by FutureCycle Press in 2021. Other books include *All These Restless Ghosts* (FutureCycle), *In the Century of Small Gestures* (Defined Providence), and *Whistle Maker* (Anhinga). He has won fellowships from the NEA, Yaddo, and the MacDowell colony and multiple awards from the PSA.

Xiaoly Li is a poet, photographer, and computer engineer who lives in Massachusetts. Her poetry is forthcoming or recently appeared in *Spillway, Spoon River Poetry Review, American Journal of Poetry, PANK, Atlanta Review, Chautauqua, Rhino, Cold Mountain Review, J Journal*, and elsewhere, including several anthologies. She has been nominated for Best of the Net twice, Best New Poets, and a Pushcart Prize.

Tom Darin Liskey spent nearly a decade working as a journalist in Venezuela, Argentina, and Brazil. His writing has appeared in *HeartWood, Live Nude Poems*, and *Driftwood Press*, as well as in a micro short story collection in novella form, *This Side of The River*. His photographs have been published in *Museum of Americana, Cultivating*, and *Midwestern Gothic*, among other publications.

Dominique Traverse Locke is an educator, prize-winning poet, and Pushcart Prize nominee from the Appalachian Mountains of southwest Virginia. She received her BA in English from Virginia Intermont College and her MFA in creative writing from Queens University of Charlotte. Dominique was named one of the "Four under Forty Notable Appalachian Writers" and has been publishing regularly since 2006.

Fabiyas M V is a writer from Orumanayur village in Kerala, India. He is the author of *Monsoon Turbulence* (Poetry Nook, US) *Shelter within the Peanut Shells* (Red Cherry Books, India) *Kanoli Kaleidoscope* (PunksWritePoemsPress, US), *Eternal Fragments* (erbacce press, UK), *Stringless Lives* (Budding Light Press, Australia), and *Moonlight and Solitude* (Raspberry Books, India). His fiction and poetry have appeared in several anthologies, magazines, and journals.

Michal Mitak Mahgerefteh is an award-winning poet and artist from Israel, living in Virginia since 1986. She is the managing editor of *Poetica Magazine* and *Mizmor Anthology* and the selecting editor for Miriam Rachimi micro-chapbook prize. Michal is currently developing DoodleMe abstract art series, created during the COVID pandemic, inspired by long walks around the city's parks and botanical gardens. Michal is the author of six chapbooks.

Lisa Suhair Majaj has authored *Geographies of Light* (Del Sol Press Poetry Prize winner) and two children's books, as well as literary analysis and creative nonfiction. She coedited three collections of essays on Arab, Arab American, and international women of color authors. Her writing has been widely published and translated into several languages and has appeared in different venues, including the 2016 exhibition *Aftermath: The Fallout of War—America and the Middle East* (Harn Museum of Art). She lives in Cyprus.

Mohini Malhotra is an international development economist, adjunct professor, and founder of a social enterprise (www.artbywomen.gallery) to promote contemporary women artists and invest in causes that better women's and girls' lives. She loves language, and her fiction has appeared in *Gravel, West Texas Literary Review, Silver Birch Press, Blink-Ink, Flash Frontier, 82 Star Review, A Quiet Courage, Writers' Center,* and several anthologies.

Natalie Mislang Mann is an educator who holds a Master of Arts in Humanities from San Francisco State University. Before being selected as a 2018 PEN America Emerging Voices fellow, she attended VONA/Voices and Tin House Summer Workshops. Her writing has appeared in *Angel City Review, The Rattling Wall,* and the anthology *Only Light Can Do That.* Natalie is currently working on a memoir based on her experiences growing up in a multi-ethnic family in the San Fernando Valley at the Bennington Writing Seminars.

Brett L. Massey is a double survivor. He survived COVID-19 and thirty years in Texas prisons. As he prepares for release, he is thankful for the second chance to rebuild his life and *live.* Something so many people didn't get. He has learned through his experience that we should live every day as if it were our last because nothing has been promised to us. Live in the present but hope for a tomorrow.

C. Liegh McInnis is a poet, short story writer, essayist, author of eight books, former editor of *Black Magnolias Literary Journal,* Prince scholar, and retired English instructor at Jackson State University. He is also a former first runner-up of the Amiri Baraka/Sonia Sanchez Poetry Award sponsored by North Carolina Agricultural and Technical State University. He is also the author of *The Lyrics of Prince* and *Brother Hollis: The Sankofa of a Movement Man.*

Kevin McLellan is the author of: *Ornitheology* (2019 Massachusetts Book Awards recipient); *Tributary; Hemispheres* (resides in special collections in the Poetry Center at the University of Arizona and the

University of Buffalo library); [*box*] (resides in the Blue Star Collection at Harvard University, MIT, the History Project and other special collections); and *Round Trip*. Kevin is also a video artist and produced the short video *Duck Hunting with the Grammarian*. He lives in Cambridge, Massachusetts. https://kevmclellan.com/

Marcelle Mentor is a faculty member at Teachers College, Columbia University. Her scholarship is grounded in Black studies, intersectional analyses, and commitment to dismantling Black racism in educational spaces. As a South African native, she teaches philosophy based on the concept of Ubuntu, a Southern African ethic that believes we are people through the existence and interaction with and from other people. She is an activist, a mother of two sons, a wife, a researcher, a scholar, and teller of stories.

E. Ethelbert Miller is a literary activist and author of two memoirs and several poetry collections. He hosts the WPFW morning radio show *On the Margin with E. Ethelbert Miller* and hosts and produces *The Scholars* on UDC-TV which received a 2020 Telly Award. Miller's latest book is *When Your Wife Has Tommy John Surgery and Other Baseball Stories*, published by City Point Press.

Elia Min is a high school senior with a growing interest in art and art history. She also advocates for climate justice in Los Angeles, her hometown. Growing up Korean American, Elia has learned to balance the two most prominent cultures in her life. She enjoys baking in her free time and often shares with friends and family.

Rayna Momen is a Black, trans poet, queer criminologist, and abolitionist, born and raised in Morgantown, West Virginia. Their creative and academic work seeks to disrupt dominant narratives and often chronicles life on the edges of society. Momen believes in people, not prisons; in love, not war; and in being able to maneuver through the world as our authentic selves.

Kenneth Moore Jr., #V-97875, was born on June 2, 1981, in Los Angeles California. As a child, he enjoyed the recreational activities of his family, such as raising pigeons, riding minibikes, and doing backflips. He has experienced many employment, and academic opportunities. He received his GED in 2019 and continued his education with Cuesta College.

Lisa Michelle Moore is a health care provider and writer living on the Canadian Prairies. Her poetry and prose have appeared in *The Cold Mountain Review, Anti-Heroine Chic, Sad Girls Lit Club,* and *The Daily Drunk.*

Aimee Nicole is a chronically ill queer poet currently residing in Rhode Island. She holds a BFA in creative writing from Roger Williams University and has been published by *Red Booth Review, The Nonconformist,* and *Voice of Eve,* among others. She enjoys attending roller derby bouts and trying desperately to win at drag bingo.

Mary K O'Melveny, a retired labor rights lawyer, lives with her wife near Woodstock, New York. Mary's award-winning poetry has appeared in many print and online journals and on national blog sites. She is the author of *A Woman of a Certain Age* and *Merging Star Hypotheses* (Finishing Line Press, 2018, 2020), *Dispatches from the Memory Care Museum* (Kelsay Books, 2021) and coauthor of the anthology *An Apple in Her Hand* (Codhill Press, 2019).

Frances Ogamba is the winner of the 2020 Kalahari Short Story Competition and the 2019 Koffi Addo Prize for Creative Nonfiction. She was a finalist for the 2019 Writivism Short Story Prize and 2019 Brittle Paper Awards for short fiction. Her fiction appears or is forthcoming in *Chestnut Review, CRAFT, The Dark Magazine, midnight & indigo, Jalada, Cinnabar Moth,* and elsewhere. She is an alumna of the Purple Hibiscus Writing Workshop taught by Chimamanda Adichie.

Blessing Omeiza Ojo is a Nigerian teacher and author. His work has been featured in various local and international anthologies. He was a

2020 semi-finalist for Jack Grapes Poetry Prize and winner of the 9th Korea-Nigeria Poetry Prize (Ambassador Special Prize). He is currently a creative writing instructor at Jewel Model Secondary School, Abuja, where he has coached winners of national and international writing prizes. When he is not reading or writing, he may be playing PES.

Robert Okaji lives in Indiana. He holds a BA in history, served without distinction in the US Navy, and once won a goat-catching contest. He is the author of multiple chapbooks, including the 2021 Etchings Press Poetry Prize winning *My Mother's Ghost Scrubs the Floor at 2 a.m.*, and his poetry has appeared or is forthcoming in *Book of Matches*, *Juke Joint*, *One Art*, *North Dakota Quarterly*, *Vox Populi*, *Indianapolis Review*, and elsewhere.

Waliyah Oladipo is a final year law student at the University of Ibadan in Nigeria. Her works have been featured in *African Writer*, *Blue Minaret*, *Kalahari Review*, and others. She works as a part-time yoga instructor.

Poet, playwright, and editor, **Linda Parsons** is the poetry editor for Madville Publishing and reviews editor for *Pine Mountain Sand & Gravel*. She is copy editor for *Chapter 16*, the literary website of Humanities Tennessee. Linda is published in such journals as *The Georgia Review*, *Iowa Review*, *Prairie Schooner*, *Southern Poetry Review*, *The Chattahoochee Review*, *Baltimore Review*, and *Shenandoah*. Her fifth poetry collection is *Candescent* (Iris Press, 2019).

Darius Atefat-Peckham's work has appeared in *Indiana Review*, *Barrow Street*, *Michigan Quarterly Review*, *Zone 3*, *The Florida Review*, *Brevity*, and elsewhere. He is the author of the chapbook *How Many Love Poems*, forthcoming from Seven Kitchens Press. His work has recently appeared in the anthology *My Shadow Is My Skin: Voices from the Iranian Diaspora* (University of Texas Press). Atefat-Peckham grew up in Huntington, West Virginia, and currently studies creative writing at Harvard College.

Bianca Alyssa Pérez was born and raised in Mission, Texas—a small southern town bordering Mexico. She is currently an MFA poetry candidate at Texas State University. Her poems have been published in *Magma Poetry UK, ReclamationATX, The Sappho Diaries* (Psst! Press), *East French Press, The New York Quarterly, Re-side Magazine,* and *The Ice Colony Anthology.* She is also the cohost of the horror podcast *Basement Girls* with writer Stephanie Grossman.

Luis Perez was born in Cuba and emigrated to the United States in 1966 as a teenager. He has been imprisoned for over five decades. With the exception of his two daughters, all of his family has died during his incarceration. Luis has self-published two books: *Man Without Country* and *Abnormal Footprint.*

Kenneth Pobo is the author of twenty-one chapbooks and nine full-length collections. Recent books include *Bend of Quiet* (Blue Light Press), *Loplop in a Red City* (Circling Rivers), and *Uneven Steven* (Assure Press). *Opening* is forthcoming from Rectos Y Versos Editions. *Lavender Fire, Lavender Rose* is forthcoming from Brick/House Books.

Steve Ramirez hosts the weekly reading series Two Idiots Peddling Poetry. A former member of the Laguna Beach Slam Team, he's also a former organizer of the Orange County Poetry Festival and former member of the Five Penny Poets in Huntington Beach. Publication credits include *Pearl, The Comstock Review, Crate, Aim for the Head* (a zombie anthology), and *MultiVerse* (a superhero anthology).

Emily Ransdell's work has been published in *Tar River Poetry, Spillway, Poet Lore, River Styx, Poetry Northwest,* and elsewhere. She has been runner-up for the *New Letters, Prime Number,* and *Ruminate* poetry prizes as well as a finalist for the *Rattle* poetry prize. She was twice featured by Ted Kooser in *American Life in Poetry.* Emily lives in Camas, Washington.

David Antonio Reyes, born and raised in El Paso, Texas, received a BA from the University of Texas at El Paso and completed his MFA in poetry at New Mexico State University. His work has appeared in *Gulf Coast, The Acentos Review, Grand Little Things, Rio Grande Review*, and *Borderzine*. He taught English composition at NMSU and El Paso Community College and currently assists students in transitioning to college in El Paso where he lives, writes, and creates music.

Christine Rhein is the author of *Wild Flight*, winner of the Walt McDonald First Book Prize in Poetry (Texas Tech University Press). Her recent work appears in *Michigan Quarterly Review, Rattle*, and *The Southern Review*. Her poems have been selected for Poetry Daily, Verse Daily, the Writer's Almanac, and for anthologies, including *Best New Poets* and *The Best American Nonrequired Reading*. A former automotive engineer, Christine lives in Brighton, Michigan. http://www.christinerhein.com

Deborah "Deby" Rodriguez is a Cuban-Colombian first-generation American. She is also a wordsmith, hypnotherapist, and psycho-spiritual educator. In her writings, Deby often uses her experiences as a queer Latina to explore themes of displacement, identity, and home. In this poem, however, she focuses instead on celebrating the connection and beauty that become available when we are present. In the midst of global crisis, her writings highlight and excavate the possibilities of hope, vulnerability, and truth.

Though a glass worker by day, **Z. S. Roe** spends his early mornings and evenings writing. He is the author of *Broken Reflections*, a poetry chapbook about life in the glass industry (published by Plan B Press). His short fiction has appeared in various publications, including *The First Line, Joypuke II*, and *Dark Moon Digest*, among others.

Maria Rouphail is the author of *Apertures* (Finishing Line Press), "New Women's Voices" series, and *Second Skin* (Main Street Rag). Emerita senior lecturer in literature (North Carolina State University), she currently serves as poetry editor of *Main Street Rag*. *All the Way to China* (Finishing Line Press, 2022), her second full-length manuscript, was a finalist in both the University of Wisconsin Brittingham and Blue Light Press competitions in 2020.

Fred Shaw was named Emerging Poet Laureate Finalist for Allegheny County in 2020. He is a graduate of the University of Pittsburgh and Carlow University, where he received his MFA. He teaches writing and literature at Point Park University and Carlow University. His first collection, *Scraping Away*, was recently published by CavanKerry Press. He lives in Pittsburgh with his wife and rescued hound dogs.

Alan Smith Soto, a resident of Jamaica Plain, Massachusetts, and a member of the Jamaica Pond Poets, was born in San José, Costa Rica. He is the author of three books of poems: *Fragmentos de alcancía* (Cambridge, 1998), *Libro del lago* (Madrid, 2014), and *Hasta que no haya luna* (Huerga y Fierro Editores, Madrid, 2021), and a translation of Robert Creeley's *Life and Death* (*Vida y muerte*; Madrid, Árdora Ediciones, 2000).

Edward Michael Supranowicz grew up on a small farm in Appalachia. He has worked a variety of jobs, most recently as a teacher in an after school program for K–6. Some of Edward's artwork has recently appeared or is forthcoming in *Another Chicago Magazine*, *Oddball Mag*, *In Parenthesis*, *Door Is a Jar*, *FishFood Magazine*, *Dream Noir*, *Penumbra*, and other literary and art magazines. Edward is also a published poet.

Jeffrey Taylor's first submitted poems won first place and runner-up in Riff Magazine's 1994 Jazz and Blues Poetry Contest. Encouraged, he continued to write and has been published in *REED Magazine*, *di-vêrsé-city*, Yale University's *The Perch*, *Gathering Storm Magazine*, *Red River Review*, *Illya's Honey*, *Enchantment of the Ordinary*, *Texas Poetry Calendar*, and *Langdon Review*. Serving as sensei (instructor) to small children and professor to graduate students has taught him humility.

Poet and playwright, **Maria James-Thiaw** has published three books, and her poems can be found in a variety of literary journals. Her prize-winning choreopoem, "Reclaiming My Time: An American Griot Project" was transformed into a Zoom play called "RMT 2.0" in 2020. While her husband was trapped overseas for five months, this mom of two survived with the help of wine, chocolate, picket sign painting, and poetry.

Christine L. Villa is a poet, children's book writer, author of *The Bluebird's Cry* (a haiku and tanka collection), founding editor and publisher of *Frameless Sky* (a short-form poetry video journal) and of Velvet Dusk Publishing for haiku and tanka chapbooks and full-length books, and an all-around creative explorer. She is also a mixed-media artist and photographer. Her poems, books, artwork, and photographs have won awards and recognition. Visit her at www.christinevilla.com.

Internationally collected artist **Richard Vyse** has shown in galleries in Manhattan and Honolulu. He has studied at the School of Visual Arts in Manhattan and taught at Pratt Institute in Brooklyn. His art has been featured in international art magazines and is in the Leslie Lohman Museum in Manhattan.

Catherine Young's writing has been nominated for the Pushcart Prize and *Best American Essays*. She worked as a national park ranger, farmer, mother, and educator. Her ecopoetry and prose is published in anthologies and journals nationally and internationally. Rooted in farm life, Catherine lives with her family in Wisconsin. Her writings and podcasts are available at http://catherineyoungwriter.com.

Jody Zellen is a Los Angeles–based artist who works in many media simultaneously. She received a BA from Wesleyan University (1983), an MFA from CalArts (1989), and an MPS (2009) from New York University's Interactive Telecommunications Program. She has exhibited nationally and internationally since 1989. Please visit www.jodyzellen .com for more information.

ABOUT THE EDITORS

Amy M. Alvarez is a poet and professor. Her work focuses on race, ethnicity, gender, regionality, nationality, and social justice. Her poetry has appeared or is forthcoming in *Ploughshares*, *Crazyhorse*, *The Missouri Review*, *Alaska Quarterly Review*, *PRISM International*, and elsewhere. She is a CantoMundo, Macondo, VONA, Furious Flower, and VCCA Fellow. Her mother is a recently retired nurse and her stepfather is an essential worker and COVID-19 survivor.

Pamela Gemme has been a social worker with the Department of Children and Families in Massachusetts for thirty-two years. Her poetry has appeared in the *Chicago Quarterly Review*, *the American Journal of Poetry*, the *Mizmor Anthology*, and many other journals and anthologies. In 2018 Pamela edited art for the *Lily Poetry Review* for their first three editions. Pamela's work is shown in galleries and on the covers of books. She is a member of the Haiku Society. Pamela is working on two poetry manuscripts and is a COVID-19 survivor.

Shana Hill is a poet and former biotechnology professional. She was quarantined during the swine flu scare in Hong Kong at a hospital with bars on its windows. She previously worked closely with patients with a rare genetic disease and also volunteered with various organizations in international settings. Her poetry has appeared in *Ocean State Review*, *Slipstream*, *San Pedro River Review*, and *the museum of americana*. Shana is the founder of Poetica Pastor, a business that assists writers in seeking publication, and is married to an essential worker.

Alexis Ivy is an outreach advocate for homeless people in Cambridge, Massachusetts. She is a recipient of the 2018 Massachusetts Cultural Council Fellowship in Poetry and her second collection of poetry, *Taking the Homeless Census* (2020), won the Saturnalia Editors Prize. Alexis was unable to work directly with the public during the pandemic as she has an underlying health condition. Once she became vaccinated, she went back to direct care.

Made in the USA
Columbia, SC
10 December 2023

28164733R00200